BECOMING STARLIGHT

BECOMING STARLIGHT

A Shared Death Journey from Darkness to Light

SHARON PRENTICE, PhD

Printed in the United States of America

First Printing, 2018

ISBN-13: 978-1-947637-94-8 print edition
ISBN-13: 978-1-947637-95-5 ebook edition

Waterside Press
2055 Oxford Ave
Cardiff, CA 92007
www.waterside.com

For the loves of my life

Because they matter

CONTENTS

A Note from the Author

I don't believe in coincidence. I believe in the serendipitous-ness of life, the sacred geometry of the universe, the surprise "How did you know?" that explodes in those unexplainable moments of pure recognition between people, in the unadulterated forces of nature that are swaying to a beat set by some unseen hand. And I believe in what may seem "corny" and old-fashioned to some—the absolute power of love that can move mountains. I've seen it, experienced it, and felt its magnificence in so many ways and in so many moments of joy as well as in moments of undeniable and unrelenting despair.

And I believe in the spiritual foundations of the world. Those foundations set the world on fire as well as quench the burning desire of the millions who yearn to tap into and understand just who we are, what we are, and where we belong in the tapestry of all life.

You found your way to *Starlight*. Somehow, in the universe of books available, you found your way to *Starlight*. Or should I say *Starlight* found you? Did you reach out and there, at your fingertips—sat *Starlight*? Or were you consciously searching for an answer to a question that seemed to have no answer—and there sat Starlight. Either way—you're here. And whatever force of nature brought you here, allow me to say, "Welcome."

Like me, you're a searcher, a researcher, an explorer, a novice guest in a world chock full of would-be experts who would have us believe that all the answers to all the questions about life and death and God and reality and truth have already been discovered, and that we need only ask for all to be revealed. If only that were true!

But I think we all know that the answers we are longing for don't come quite so easily, and very rarely do they come at the behest of some "expert" who just wants to "show you the way." Sometimes it takes years, and those years are full of soul-searching journeys and adventures which, oftentimes, lead to life-changing events that leave us breathless with mouths gaping and hands sweating.

So—here you are—holding *Becoming Starlight* in your hands. Perhaps you are looking for something in particular or just looking for something that "seems different." Or perhaps Starlight spoke to you as it spoke to me on that one particular night.

Know this one thing as truth—you are part of something so powerful, so magnificent, so all-consuming and loving, that separation from "all that is" is simply never an option. Shall humanity discover its true essence in what you now hold in your hands? Is it there...in Starlight? Are we there...in Starlight?

Only time...and faith...will tell...

FOREWORD

"The eye through which I see God is the same
eye through which God sees me"
—Meister Eckert

*B*ecoming *Starlight*, Dr. Sharon Prentice's gripping
account of her spiritual quest, shines new light on
numerous significant aspects of the mystery of the afterlife.

In her book, Dr. Prentice describes her shared
death experience, a profound episode of transcendent
consciousness that has some characteristics of the near
death experience, and yet the person going through it
is not ill or injured; rather, it occurs in connection with
the death of someone else. Dr. Prentice's experience was
tied to the passing of her husband.

I want to highlight four specific ways in which
this book makes important contributions. First,
Dr. Prentice's account of her shared death experience
is vital because the SDE is a phenomenon that prom-
ises to reshape rational inquiry into near death experiences. Secondly, she provides a memorably vivid picture
of the ineffability—or indescribability—that is almost

universally reported by people with mystical visions during a near death experience. Thirdly, her description of the process of grief and its relationship to mysteries concerning the afterlife will comfort readers who are mourning the loss of loved ones. Lastly, Dr. Prentice has a refreshing take on God, one that coincides with what has been mentioned to me by hundreds of people with near death experiences. I want to discuss each of those four topics in turn:

Becoming Starlight is in the vanguard of a series of works that together are a breakthrough in understanding the biggest question of existence. In fact, Dr. Prentice's shared death experience is a good example of an event that disrupts and overturns the standard model of debating about near death experiences. This model goes back to the Greek philosophers, Plato and Democritus, both of whom wrote on the occasional events in which somebody revived after apparent death and told of a journey to the other side. Plato took these stories seriously as an indication of an afterlife, but Democritus expressed a different opinion. Democritus held that everything was made up of tiny invisible bits of material substance that he called atoms, so he reasoned that even after an apparent death there is some residual biological activity in the body, which, he said, explained the stories of people who said they went to the other side.

Today, unlike in Plato's and Democritus' world, revival after apparent death is a common occurrence. There are many more people in 2018 who survive to tell us about their near death experiences, yet we still debate the meaning of near death experiences according to that same old format shared by Plato and Democritus. Some scholars look at near death experiences as indicators of an afterlife and others look at near death experiences as the result of oxygen deprivation in the brain of a critically ill patient. Of course, oxygen deprivation could not account for Dr. Prentice's experience since she was not the person who was dying. Therein lies the SDE's significance in the debate.

I have interviewed many hundreds of people who reported profound shared death experiences, and believe these events are taking us to the threshold of revolutionary new rational methods of investigating the afterlife.

Becoming Starlight pinpoints the single most crucial factor in rational inquiry into this vastly important question of the afterlife: ineffability. Dr. Prentice states that there are simply no words to describe the experience of one's soul slipping over to another framework of existence, a realm of sheer love and light. The language barrier which she so firmly delineates is the primary obstacle that prevents us from making sense of what awaits us when we die. Dr. Prentice has worked with me and other participants in this work in beginning to break down the language barrier; soon we will have exciting new linguistic and conceptual means to talk to one another about the afterlife.

The book will also bring comfort to those who are feeling unrelenting grief over lost loved ones. Dr. Prentice's honest, soul-wrenching descriptions of her grief over her daughter and husband will be helpful to many readers. Putting grief into words is a very difficult thing to do; I admire her for her willingness to talk about the horrible pain of grief while offering hope for a resolution.

Finally, Dr. Prentice's graphic account of her tumultuous relationship with God is a real pearl; she takes a relational view of God rather than a belief-based one. I love her outpouring of raw emotions that seem to be almost universal among those who experience a direct personal encounter with God. The orientation of people who have near death experiences typically shifts from a religious concept of God to a personal relationship, much like friendship. I think this book can really help those who are still affected with a fear of a vengeful God that is rooted in severe religious ideologies.

Dr. Prentice's book is a thought-provoking advance that can help bring about progress toward rational enlightenment on the afterlife question. What you will read here opens many new avenues for thinking about humankind's deepest mystery. Hold onto your hat when you read this book.

Becoming Starlight is truly sensational; anyone who is seriously interested in the question of life after death should read it.

—Raymond Moody, M.D., Ph.D.,
author of *Life After Life*, *Reunions*,
and *Glimpses of Eternity*

ACKNOWLEDGMENTS

To Dr. Raymond Moody, the reigning mentor of all those who came before my Starlight night and those who will come after, the man who is considered the father of the NDE and the SDE, I stand up and applaud you. You made it possible for those of us who have experienced these Spiritual Blessings to understand them. You explained to me that I wasn't alone, that there were others struggling as I had struggled to make sense of it all … and you gave me the peace of mind I needed to believe all that I knew to be true and valid—were, indeed, true and valid. Through your constant research and dedication, you have helped many around the globe come to terms with their experience. You have made it possible for others to join in and continue on with the very important work necessary on the subject of the NDE and the SDE. Your courses on this subject were instrumental to my understanding of the actual history—dating back to Plato's time—of the true nature of these experiences. Your kind and gentle ways are so telling of your nature and I thank you for your efforts on behalf of those of us who have finally come out of the shadows to tell our stories. Without your guidance and encouragement, it would have been impossible to tell the story about my Starlight night. I am forever grateful to you, not just because of your amazing dedication to a field that is constantly in search of meaning but also because of your courage and resolute strength of character.

Becoming Starlight would not exist in this form if it weren't for the urgings of my Spiritual provocateur, the late Dr. Wayne Dyer. Wayne convinced me to write this memoir one day as we were sitting on the floor in the lobby of a hotel sharing a banana. His words rang loud and true in my mind then, as they do now: "Tell the story, Sharon. Always tell the story." His guidance and support were instrumental in the telling of my Starlit night and I, along with millions around the globe, still grieve the death of this remarkable man. One of my last conversations with Wayne is so telling of his true Spirit and his kind and gentle demeanor. When I asked, "Do you think Steve and Stephanie will know about *Becoming Starlight*?" he answered, "They already do." Thank you, Wayne, for your unwavering and always-present lessons about the true nature of our lives.

So many amazing families have spent time in my life—it feels as if they *are* family and, actually, many have become family. To say that I have been Blessed by them is an understatement of massive proportion. They have allowed me to be with them during the most difficult and grievous moments of their lives and they have trusted me with their loved ones in the last moments of their lives.

They have shared their love, their hopes and dreams, their complete devastations and nightmares with me and have honored me in so many ways with their tears and their laughter. They have ripped open their lives and shared the good, the bad, and the ugly with me. For that, I can never thank them enough, and for showering me with their love and concern at the same time they are losing their lives or the lives of their loved ones—there can be no words adequate enough to express my thoughts. These people are a rare breed and I have learned so much about courage and inner strength from them. Sometimes, it's very difficult for them when I walk through that door day after day—they know what that means—but the acceptance given to me is more than extraordinary and I can only pray they know how much they mean to me. They are such a part of my Spirit and I know we will walk together for years to come as friends who have shared those most precious of all moments—the life and death struggle we all must, one day, prepare for. To them I say, "I love you" and I will remember each one of you, by name, for the rest of my life.

And to my spiritually Blessed friend, Dr. Michael Abidin—thank you for your ever present support and love. You are and forever will be part of my life in a way that others simply do not or cannot understand. You have managed to catch a glimpse of eternity that few others even aspire to, and your gifts, which you give so freely to others, are an inspiration to all who have the opportunity to call you friend. I am blessed to call you my friend.

To Anne Cole Norman—there are no words in existence to fully express my gratitude and love for Anne Cole Norman, editor extraordinaire. Anne was with me from the very beginning before one word was ever written on the page of some notebook that had the word "Starlight" emblazoned on the cover. She survived all the incarnations of *Starlight* and her gentleness and concern for *Starlight* remaining true to its purpose was always up front and center. Her tender and supportive manner was evident in her editing as she very carefully tried to steer me away from the bleeding vulnerability that came through in the very first page ever written. Her support and guidance and expert editing were a saving grace for me and I know Anne and I will be friends and "partners in crime" for the rest of our days. Thank you, Anne, for giving me your best. Working with a novice writer can never be easy for someone as experienced and talented as Anne but, somehow, she managed to survive me and, because of her expertise, *Becoming Starlight* emerged the way Wayne always thought it would—we told the story.

I also wish to thank graphic designer, Ken Fraser, of Impact Book Designs. Ken believed in *Starlight* before he had ever even read a word of the story. Our conversations seemed as if we had known each other for years and it didn't take more than a moment in time for us to be on the same page as far as the cover design for *Starlight*. Ken understood the entire premise and accepted *Starlight* from our initial conversation as something impactful and real. He took Kristen Dawn's Dreamscape, and, with his expert skills and his intuitive leanings, crafted a stunning cover. Thank you, Ken, for your belief in those things that must be taken on faith.

And to Kristen Dawn—a Soul Mate in this amazing universe, for her design, which serves as the inspiration for the cover of this book. From the very inception of this project, I envisioned, in my Soul, a picture that would express my Starlit night in such a way that readers could imagine themselves among the stars. Almost immediately, I came across Kristen's design and I knew she must have had some type of experience to be able to design something so completely representative of my night among the stars—so I wrote to her. I wrote to her asking permission to use her design because nothing else would do. Nothing! It seemed impossible that a complete stranger could have visually "designed" my Starlit night so perfectly—but that is exactly what she had accomplished! When we connected, the story she shared with me—the story of just how her design came into existence—left me speechless. It was simply extraordinary—and it was then that I knew she had been sent to me from "that place." Kristen designed this amazing work from a dream. She explains it this way: "I was lost in a huge field and no matter which way I turned, I couldn't find my way home. I felt as if I would die out there in the night. It felt as if I was lost for all eternity. I eventually just gave up trying to find a way out and lay down in the grass, crying. I began to sing myself a song—not a real song but one I made up. When I was ready to give up … to just die … She came to me from among the stars. The stars were swirling around my head and then exploded into an entire cosmos. I didn't know if she was God or Mother Nature coming to me...but then Her face became clear and that's all I remember." For sharing your talent, and your most intimate moments of fear, I thank you...as does my Starlit night. How amazing is the connectedness of the Universe and how God works His magic!!

And to Kenneth Kales, Editorial Director and Managing Editor of Waterside Press–a big thank you! Your kind and gentle patience was much appreciated throughout this process. As I'm sure you discovered early on—I am somewhat computer illiterate! I am a talker, a counselor, and I "do" face to face—not email to email or text to text. Some tell me I need to come into this century and give up my face to face preferences but, for me, that is quite an impossibility. For your persever-ance and understanding, I thank you. You never once made me feel anything except important and your help proved to be invaluable. Thank you, Kenneth, for your kind and generous Soul.

And to Bill Gladstone of Waterside Productions. What can I possibly say about Bill Gladstone? This man took a chance on a totally unknown, unproven, first-time author who had absolutely no knowledge or experience in the world of publishing. For Bill to sign on as my agent still sends me into reams of laughter as I consider his stature and reputation as an agent to some of the very people whose books line the shelves of my office and my home. He took a chance on me and I will be forever grateful to him for his guidance and his patience with all my questions, emails, texts and down-right naiveté of the publishing empire he presides over. To have him as part of my life and to have him believe in *Starlight* is one of my most amazing experiences—one I cannot explain in terms that even I understand completely. He is a man of integrity and the truth knows it has a home within him. I thank you, Bill—for giving this "newbie" the opportunity to share the story of the night where magnificent love was found. Your generous and kind words about *Starlight* live in me and make the vulnerability inherent in this memoir well worth any challenges that may come my way. I am forever grateful.

And finally—to my family. It's because of you that I breathe. You are my very heart. For my son—I will be your memory as you are my Spirit. You are the reason I live and survived. You are the joy that exists in me and the joy that lived in your father's heart. That can never be changed or forgotten regardless of the passage of time. You are the reason *Starlight* was written. It is your legacy of love from your dad, given to me for you. No purer love ever existed.

And for Jerry—you came to me during the empty times—not as a filler to plump up the empty spaces but as a Blessing to light the way back to life and love in the here and now. Your constancy and devotion to me during the writing of *Becoming Starlight* was nothing short of an overwhelming dedication to the truth of what we have built together. Never once did you falter and question our love while reading my words about the life I lived in that "before" time. Your belief in me and in *Starlight* served as an ever-present inspiration to tell my story. Your tears and your "I'm so sorry that all happened to you" have only made me love you more. I am indeed Blessed to have you by my side. Thank you, my love, for your abiding concern and care and for believing so wholeheartedly in everything I do.

And, finally—to Steve and Stephanie. This is your story. Why? Because you were here. Because you matter. Because you taught me about life and love. And because, without you... my life, as it is, would not exist. I know you wait for me within Starlight. And I will be back. Thank you, my loves, for loving me as much as you did.

And, above all else, I thank God for His many Blessings in my life. He is the maker of *Becoming Starlight* as it was His hand that guided mine. This is His story of life and love and forgiveness. For that, I am eternally "Starlight."

INTRODUCTION

Have you ever lost someone you loved and then struggled with the question, "Where is he?" or "How can
she just be gone?" Following the death of a loved one,
have you ever thought, "This can't be all there is!" These
age-old queries about the physical/emotional/spiritual
puzzle are asked thousands and thousands of times each
day worldwide. The search for answers brings so many
of us to the brink of an immeasurable abyss, and then
leaves us gasping for air and begging for that one sen-
tence that will put our hearts to rest. But just where do
we go for that answer? Does it lie within the Church and
the clergy?

For centuries, people turned to the church for comfort in hopes of discovering some new revelation but
oftentimes, that revelation was simply "God knows best."
Taken on faith, some found the peace they were searching for in that simple statement of fact. But those of us
who may not have the faith "that moves mountains"—we
are left shaken and alone. That very "aloneness" becomes
the impetus for a journey into realms not considered
before—unknown, sometimes frightening, but always

transformative. Enter the Shared Death Experience (SDE). Everyone absolutely everywhere who is searching for the answer to life-and-death questions runs head-on into the SDE and the Near Death Experience (NDE).

The SDE. Most people know of, or know someone who has experienced, a NDE, but very few have heard of the SDE. The SDE is similar to the NDE except that it occurs not to the person who is dying, but to their loved one who is physically well. That person could be sitting right next to their loved one, or sitting across the room, or even be across the globe unaware of the impending death of someone they love. They could be sound asleep or wide awake – makes no difference. Location or activity level is of no consequence to the SDE. That person, the loved one, is "invited along" to witness the aftermath of physical death. The invitation extended has no RSVP—the person accompanying the dying individual can neither accept nor refuse—they are just "taken" or "given" the experience.

Although the SDE and the NDE initially present themselves as new phenomena, seekers soon come to understand that these phenomena are as old as humanity itself. They simply were not discussed openly.

One of the first documented SDE's took place during World War I, according to a 2014 CNN article, *Beyond Goodbye*. A German soldier named Karl Skala was in a foxhole when an artillery shell exploded, killing a fellow soldier.

He felt the soldier slump into his arms and die, then felt himself being drawn up with his friend, above their bodies and above the battlefield. He was able to look down and see himself holding his friend, then saw a bright light that he felt himself approaching with his friend. Then he returned, uninjured, to his own body.

People hardly ever reported SDE's until very recently, when all over the world, seemingly at the same time, individuals began to open up and willingly share their spiritual experiences.

Within this global Spiritual Awakening, those who've had SDE's are actively seeking a new way of "being" in this world. The ancient "Who am I?" question has resurfaced with a vengeance—and a new twist. No longer are people satisfied to get their answer from the status quo of organized religion and the lessons contained therein. The old "just believe this because I say so" is no longer valid for the person on a quest for spiritual enlightenment; the one who wants to know exactly where we fit into the tapestry that binds the universe together.

The Spiritual journeys of today are taking people away from the traditional models of religion and plunging them into deeper, more confusing waters where the mystics alone seem to tread. Alternative models of discovery such as meditation, hypnotism, conversational prayer, mysticism, Spiritual Counseling, Reiki—and so many others—are playing a deeper role than ever before in the journey to discover who we are and what we are in relation to a God that many of us feel alienated from and empty of. People are searching for a connectedness to God, to the Universe, and to each other in a way that has us looking to the stars for answers. We seem to be combining the spiritual values of all humanity in an effort to arrive "home"—that place where our lost loved ones wait for us and where we all fit together as one unifying presence within Creation Itself.

The common bond here lies in humanity's current lifting of the veil to discover our true Spiritual identity, our place in this vast universe, and our transcendence of the five senses we all must live within in this physical plane of existence. Everyone wants to know, "Is there someone else out there like me? Do they know? What have they found?" The need to know is more than just a "need"—it is an essential. They want to know and are eager to share and learn from experiences—even if the experience is not their own. This quest for knowledge, along with the discoveries that wake us up, are catalysts for people to open up and share with the world events that they were afraid to share before because of fear of rejection and ridicule.

The events they describe are full of a strife—and sometimes rage—that is difficult to explain. *Becoming Starlight* is one of those stories. It is a story with the type of pitfalls that accompany much of mankind on the journey through existence. Deeply embedded in *Starlight* is an ongoing war with faith and hope and with God—a war most of us have experienced or will experience in our lifetimes.

Becoming Starlight is a story that has been written, in one way or another, since the beginning of time. The war between life and death—who lives and who dies and why they die—is at the heart of this deeply personal experience. It's a life-and-death struggle with spiritual darkness and loss of faith. It is a story not unlike the stories of anyone who has loved and lost, grieved and sorrowed, felt anguish and rage, fallen from Grace and questioned the very existence of God. The specifics are different, but the humanity splattered on the human soul is the same as that of any life lived fully. Some find redemption more easily than I. It took a complete fall from grace for me to be awakened from the trauma and darkness that had found its way into my life, and it took an unexpected encounter – a SDE—to bring me into the arms of God, where I finally found the solace and understanding that I had yearned for.

Annie Cap told the story of her SDE in her 2011 book *Beyond Goodbye: An Extraordinary Story of a Shared Death Experience.* In 2004, Cap got a call that her mother had suddenly fallen ill and been taken to the hospitalized. Born in the U.S., Cap was living in England at the time. Within days, her mother's major organs began to shut down.

Cap had been unable to catch a flight back home, but one day while she was still in London meeting with a business contact, she struggled to breathe, despite being in perfectly good health. The episode lasted almost half an hour, and her thoughts turned to her mother.

Cap called her mother's hospital room and learned that her mother was also gasping for air, on the brink of death. Her mother died during the phone call, and today Cap believes that she had a SDE with her mother.

Penny Sartori was a nurse for seventeen years in the Intensive Therapy Unit of a major British hospital.

During that time, she had many experiences with dying patients, including what she characterizes as SDE's.

"I have documented cases where people who were present at the bedside of their dying loved one suddenly found themselves participating in a transcendent experience of a partial journey into death," Sartori wrote on her blog

"I have also documented cases where miles away from their dying loved one people have suddenly and inexplicably been overwhelmed with intense emotion – this coincided with the death of a loved one."

Most SDE's are tales of great love that become—as happens when death enters the picture—telling accounts of tremendous struggle for survival, not only physically, but spiritually, as well, in the aftermath of death. It is a transformative event that leaves one shaken to the very core, confused and questioning everything one had believed to be true about the universe.

Becoming Starlight is one of those stories. It is an account, my account, of a Soul's journey that leads to an unraveling of a lifetime of beliefs about God and our very existence in this universe.

Knowing that one is not alone – that *we* are not alone—is at the heart of the SDE. More and more, people all over the globe are sharing their unique and spiritually transformative SDE stories.

Raymond Moody, the man *The New York Times* calls "the father of the Near Death Experience," wrote the book *Glimpses of Eternity* (2009) about SDE's. (He is also the author of the 1975 book *Life After Life*, which sold 13 million copies, for which he interviewed 150 people who had undergone NDE's.)

"I first heard such a shared-death experience from one of my professors of medicine," Moody wrote in an article for the website *Natural Transitions.* "This doctor had the unfortunate duty of trying to resuscitate her own mother... She told me that when she felt her mother die, she found herself floating out of her body and viewing the scene from above. She saw her own physical body and the now-deceased body of her mother down below... [her mother] receded into an intensely brilliant, white light... Then the light was gone... She found herself back in her own physical body, standing beside the deceased body of her mother."

After this experience, Moody began to hear similar stories. He noted multiple key elements of the SDE, all of which are similar to those of the near-death experience:

1. They see a light
2. They see the deceased relatives of the dying, coming to meet them
3. They see the spirit of the dying "rising up" from the body, described as a "misty glow" or greyish cloud"
4. They sometimes participate in the "panoramic life review" of the dying person, in which the dying person's entire life flashes by
5. They feel the dimensions of the room around them transforming from a square/rectangle to an hourglass shape

As with *Life After Life* much of *Glimpses of Eternity* is based on anecdotal evidence, which has caused the scientific community to dismiss it as unreliable.

However, it's important to note that the anecdotal evidence is coming from people experiencing anoxia, the standard medical explanation for near-death hallucinations. It also comes in large part from medical personnel, who don't personally know the dying person's relatives or life details. This makes it more difficult to discount them.

A project called the Shared Death Experience Study (shareddeathstudy.org) collects SDE stories from all over the world, in as many languages as possible. It defines SDE's as "common death-bed visions and near-death experiences that family, friends and caregivers witness along with a person who is dying." The project's founders have discovered that key elements of the SDE are in line with those that Raymond Moody has cited in the past:

1. Room shape changes.
2. Bystander(s) views mist rising from dying person's body.
3. Dying person telepathically communicates with bystander(s).
4. Bystander(s) leaves their body.
5. Bystander(s) engulfed by intensely bright light that feels like absolute love.
6. Life review about dying person, the bystander(s) or both.

7. Bystander(s) accompanies the dying person through a tunnel to 'heaven'.
8. Bystander(s) views or is otherwise aware of deceased relatives and friends in the room of dying person.

The ongoing worldwide research into the subject of the SDE is changing our perception of death as well as our relationship with God Himself. It's helping us better understand the massive Spiritual awakening and rethinking of life and death that is occurring, seemingly at the same time, on a global level. Researchers from all disciplines seem to be waking up to the fact that there are questions that need answers, and this has resulted in major research centers and universities focusing on the SDE phenomenon. The study of the SDE lays waste to the neurological theories that abound in some medical communities and is becoming one of the most discussed and relevant issues in the search for truth and awareness of Being.

Researchers at the University of California at Santa Barbara (UCSB) are conducting a study in conjunction with a project called the Shared Crossing Research Initiative (the aim of which is "to promote a more conscious, connected, and loving end-of-life experience") to demonstrate whether or not it will one day be possible to intentionally orchestrate a SDE. The UCSB team is being directed by Michael Kinsella, President of the Religion, Experience and Mind Lab Group, and funded by UC Riverside's Science of Immortality project.

The study of SDE's can be daunting due to the lack of scientifically validated and "proven" results. Relying on anecdotal reporting of both NDE and SDE phenomena has never been fully accepted by the medical or hard and fast scientific community. In our world of "just the facts" we tend to dismiss anything that can't be scientifically reproduced in a lab; some think the SDE is merely the moaning of a grieving heart.

What these skeptics fail to understand, however, is that, similar to empirical, observational evidence, anecdotal evidence can be—and has been—invaluable to the body of knowledge surrounding death and dying. It must be remembered that in science, evidence is never considered proven true until further evidence is observed that contradicts the hypothesis/theory/interpretation of previous evidence. The concept of absolute proof is not part of science. It is valid in mathematics and law but not in science in its strictest sense. Empirical and anecdotal evidence are two of the measures that maintain science as always self-correcting and as a means of study and continued learning.

Consider, for instance, the quark and the Higgs boson particle (aka the "God particle"). The extraordinary physicists who populated the Manhattan Project had no knowledge of the Higgs boson – they may not have even imagined anything like it. What today is widely accepted as the newest and best in science changes daily with new concepts and new ideas only dreamed of by seekers of "truth."

Just a few short years ago, the NDE was considered nonsense, which, in light of the newest research, has left many scientists red-faced and chagrined. There will be a similar occurrence with the SDE when we come to recognize that just because a phenomenon is not readily reproducible does not make it nonsensical. As we develop more and better methods for researching what is now considered empirical or anecdotal, I believe we will make huge gains in this arena based on the mountains of reports available to researchers. What is not realized today will be realized tomorrow.

Every single report of a SDE has elements within it that speak to its transformative nature; it is an essential part of the puzzle that will lead us to a better understanding of the universe in which we all live and breathe. Quarks today—but tomorrow? Parallel dimensions? Overlapping universes? We must never mistake the human discoveries of the past or today as the absolute and final truth. Standing still is not an option.

The research into the SDE is both promising and provocative. And yet, it remains intimate and personal for those of us who have had these experiences. Scientists are opening their research doors, ushering in these events as research-worthy, and finding them provocative, curious, and somewhat mind-bending only serves to promote *more* research. Being taken into the world of Spirit is difficult for some hard-nosed scientists but I have seen even the most clinical, fact-based academic wipe away a tear as he/she thought of someone they loved—and lost—and remembered a "story' that was told about something "strange" that occurred when death came to claim their loved one, a story that was either discounted or ridiculed and never spoken of in "polite" society. I have discovered that everyone has a story—everyone.

And now these "everyone's" are sharing their stories. As am I. Why now? Why do I share this story now? In truth, I have shared my story for years with family, friends, colleagues, patients and their families—and with strangers who became seekers on their own journey of discovery. There are so many of us in the world who are in pain. Physical pain is one thing; emotional and spiritual pain is something altogether different that requires a very specific prescription for healing. And therein lies the reason those of us who have had NDE's or SDE's share these experiences.

I share with my patients to help them replace fear with hope; with their families to help them grab hold of faith—perhaps lost but hoped for; with those who cross my path in need of the stuff that sets their Soul on fire again; with those who need to remember and find their way back home again; and finally, with those who have lost and grieved and stumbled and fallen. Giving my Starlight experience to someone in need takes away the vulnerability that is intrinsic in sharing these experiences – when vulnerability morphs into strength, Starlight wins!

So—are you ready to begin? May I take you there?

Let me tell you a story........

CHAPTER 1:
UNLIKELY BEDFELLOWS

We were at war—as a nation, as communities, and as individuals. Every day, thousands of fathers and sons were waking up in a far-off land that few could even point to on a map. Wives and children were glued to their television sets as they listened intently for the strange-sounding name of some city that their loved one had mentioned in their last letter home. It was becoming a national obsession to wait for the news reports with the tally of the "count"—those who had given their lives on any particular day—and then, pray that some "uniform" didn't come knocking on their door, smileless and solemn. Here at home, college students were protesting the war even as hundreds of body bags were piled onto planes bound for home and flag-draped coffins continued to arrive at Andrews Air Force Base in Virginia.

Classrooms were empty most days as students and professors gathered outside on the quad to "discuss, debate and criticize" the current political leadership—questioning every decision that seemed to be in direct opposition to the desires of the "intellectuals" on campus. The debates and protests were constant, loud, and unnerving when opposing sides would clash and tempers flared. The college community, taken as a whole, relished the news stories that would put them front and center in the minds of the public—garnering grants from private corporations and individuals that were, in that moment, not in the political administration that held office, the one that had the power to make law. Here, in this place, sitting on the sidelines of war was not an option.

That was college, that was duty, that was expected.

I was part of that.

Not far from the university, the Marines, jet pilots, sailors, and soldiers were going about their business, trying to ignore the rantings of the students that could be heard for miles around. But the use of bullhorns and megaphones on streets that led to the military bases made it impossible for anyone to ignore the protests. The gates of the military installations were closed and protected by armed guards who were none too friendly to the screeching students who hurled obscenities at them. Knowing they were despised for their lifestyles, both sides jeered at the other—the guards laughed at and mocked the student protestors; the students spat at and cursed the guards. Eventually, though, tempers would fade to fatigue, the guards would retire to their gates and the students would retreat back into their privileged world.

He was part of that.

I was the daughter of a career Air Force officer who'd served as a jet pilot and an intelligence officer. At nineteen, I was seeking freedom from the disciplined life I was expected to live. I wanted to be involved somehow in the upheaval – so I became a helper, a gopher of sorts, staying on the uninhabited sidelines. I played at student protest from a distance—immersing myself in the college culture of the day in practical and non-threatening ways. I stayed close to the bohemian, jean-wearing, longhaired, quasi-intellectual, seemingly introspective radical poet types who ran rampant on every college campus in existence. My days and nights were filled with writing poetry, readings at the local "head" shop, and the incessant ramblings of wanna-be philosophers, as life began to repeat itself in the same fashion day after day. My rebellion against the disciplined life I had lived was actually quite boring! But exiting this life wasn't an option—the demands of my heart were stubbornly fixated on my finding a different way of life for myself—anything except the life of a "military brat."

Yes, I dabbled in protest life, but I still had enough "military" in me to know the difference between dishonorable and honorable action and behavior. I vowed to express only those thoughts and behaviors that were mine and not fall prey to the more radical notions that circled around me every day. I told myself this as often as possible. As much as I wanted to rebel, respect and honor still meant a great deal to me—and that respect and honor had formed the foundational touchstones of our home. My dad's very life was built around—and based on—integrity and honor. Dishonoring him would have been a tragic mistake—and one I could never consider making.

He was the son of a career Naval Petty Officer and had followed closely in his father's footsteps. Neat, clean cut, and polite to a fault, he spent his days on a guided missile destroyer creating electronic warfare for use in protecting our country from foreign enemies. He was completely "military" and had no intention of ever leaving the service for civilian life. His girl "back home" reflected his preference for the well-coiffed, well-behaved, well-dressed girl who was always in heels and lipstick. Not one to buck the system—but one who had gained the reputation for complete honesty under pressure—he was a rising star among his fellow officers. He had no desire to attract anything into his life that didn't fit the mold he had so carefully formed—a mold he knew would lead him to the highest ranks in his field. He was a perfectionist and took great pride in his accomplishments. He told himself he needed a wife, a partner that could successfully hold a teacup and not leave a lipstick stain on the Commanding Officer's cups at the Officers' club or during the many events that "she" would host as his wife. His life was pre-planned and non-negotiable.

But The King's Head Inn had different plans—for both of us. This bar, the heart of the university, sat on a strip of concrete directly across from the main campus. It was the hangout of choice both at night and during the day. Its siren call could be heard round the clock and drew students and professors alike at all hours. Many a time, a student skipping class would run into the professor whose class they had just cut—and would share a beer or a coke and discuss the agenda of the day's lecture. During the week, the Inn could be described as "tame" but the weekends ushered in an entirely different aspect of student life—the frat guys, sorority sisters, jocks, rebels, the intellectually "chosen" ones, the professors, the freaks, the druggies—everyone had their place at the Inn. People would start out bunched together in little factions, but this separation of "types" disappeared into the night as beer and pot were shared freely and openly. It was the Inn. It just all fit together somehow. We all belonged to the Inn—and it belonged to us.

Then he walked in. He simply swung wide the door and entered our Inn as if he was part of it—part of all this that had been so carefully crafted. He was in full dress uniform—being from a military family, I recognized the uniform at once and couldn't help but wonder just why he and his friends were in full dress. Three of them, standing at the door as if they expected the room to salute them or clear a path because "they" had arrived—they just stood there surveying the room. It was odd and disquieting. They didn't belong here, but there they stood. He, looking strong and defiant, confident and commanding, even as they were glared at by a roomful of unkempt, unwashed, hippie-ish type masqueraders. He seemed to relish the attention directed at him and his fellow officers. The comments whispered and shouted throughout the room did little to ruffle their demeanors—especially his.

The shouts from my table, in particular, were sarcastic and unwelcoming and, as I looked up to see the effect this was having on them, I saw his eyes. His eyes were locked on me. It was then I noticed something else. He held his head up high and proud, never dropping his eyes in an attempt to "hide" his face or cover his response to the ongoing verbal attacks. I found myself being drawn to this man with the almond-shaped eyes that seemed to be fixated on me now. I wondered if he was looking for "cover" somehow or if he recognized the "military" in me. As I looked into his eyes, I saw in them something unexpected—his eyes were smiling. Interesting, I thought. I most obviously wasn't his type, and even if I was, I most definitely was not interested. I looked away and tried to forget the image of the man who now filled my thoughts but was finding that impossible. Engaging in conversation with my friends seemed a foolhardy endeavor, as every word spoken just didn't seem to register in my brain. This man needed to leave.

But he didn't leave. His bravado knew no boundary as he approached my table, grabbed a chair, and sat down opposite me. "The name is Steve...and you are beautiful." I was stunned into absolute silence. Sitting there, in my bell-bottom jeans, flowing blouse, and funky platform shoes—I was the very picture of everything he was not. My hair was un-styled, wild and free—and when it fell into my face, he reached across the table and brushed it from my eyes. I had no words for this man who had no compunction about invading my personal space.

To say I was disturbed would be quite an understatement. I rose from the table and simply walked away, making a beeline for the bar.

He didn't follow. Sitting there with my friends, he began some kind of animated conversation but in no time at all, they rose to join me and left him alone at the table.

As we left the Inn, I glanced back at the now empty table and couldn't help but wonder whether the almond eyes that had stared at me were now staring at someone else. His image refused to leave my mind and I found myself smiling. Wondering if I would ever see this man again, I half-heartedly joined in the night's activities until around 2am. When I finally reached home, I fell into bed and hoped my dreams wouldn't be full of him.

A few weeks later, after that one chance meeting, he returned to the Inn, found my friends, talked them into giving him my name and address—and he drove to my home. He knocked on my door, introduced himself to my dad with a handshake and said one simple thing: "Hello Sir. My name is Steve and, if it's alright with you, I am going to marry your daughter." My Dad's response: "Well, good luck with that, son."

I wasn't home during this exchange, but when I got back and heard what had happened, I was irritated at this guy's entire attitude. Marry me? He told my dad he was going to marry me? I didn't even know him—yet I was still drowning in his eyes—curious...

It would never work, I told myself. We'd be the most mismatched couple on the planet. In fact I kept telling myself that right up to the point where, a week later, I climbed into his car to go out to dinner.

So began a relationship that was never supposed to be. We were two mismatched Souls breaking all the rules, overcoming all the objections, and somehow finding that common ground that leaves you wanting for more. And we both wanted more.

College student and warfare specialist—we didn't fit in with either one's group of friends. We tried—and failed—to become part of what and where we came from, but neither one of us felt comfortable trying to fit into a box that had definitive and unyielding dimensions. Forging our own life, according to our own beliefs, came so easily and naturally—it just felt "right."

I discovered, almost from that first moment in The Inn, that this man was incredibly kind and gentle. We would walk for hours on end through First Landing State Park and marvel at the Spanish moss that hung from the trees that seemed to erupt from the center of the earth. They filled the sky and spread throughout the landscape, creating a fairyland of sorts. The beauty of that place was matched only by the gentleness of the man who held my hand and spoke to me about his dreams for our future. We both knew we would be married, long before the word "marriage" was even spoken. Thinking back to our first meeting, I would often laugh out loud and remark to him "What on earth were you doing there?" His answer was always the same "I was looking for you."

As the weeks and months passed, we spent as much time together as possible. He became part of my family and my dad came to love him as the son he never had. I used to complain that my dad cared more about Steve than he did about me—a statement that would elicit a "Well, could be, ya know!" or "Don't screw this up"—something I couldn't do even if I wanted to. We understood each other on some level that didn't need explanation—we just knew that somehow, we fit.

We lived each day as it came. I would attend class—every class. The Inn held little for me now so cutting class didn't result in the same "playing hooky" excitement that it once did. I didn't fit there anymore. He would retreat into the darkness of his destroyer and close the heavy door behind him, hiding him and his work from the outside world. I never asked what he did. I knew enough to understand that what he was involved with was something he couldn't talk about. I had learned from my dad and his experiences as an intelligence officer that sometimes there would be secrets that must remain secrets. But each night we would come together and, even if we spent the hours just sitting at home watching repeats of *I Love Lucy* episodes, it was enough. Whatever we did, it was enough to just be together.

In October, he received orders to ship out. He was leaving for Guantanamo Bay in Cuba and would be gone for two months. Realizing I had become exactly what I had tried to not become—and that a military life loomed in front of me—I discovered that it was exactly what I wanted. I laughed at myself for trying to change the inevitability of what was to be my life as a military wife. And I found I had no regrets at all.

I knew I would miss Steve terribly while he was gone but I would just concentrate on my studies and maybe make what my dad wanted of me—Dean's list! When the day came for him to leave, I stood on the dock with the wives and girlfriends of those on board and waved—just like the others next to me who were holding crying babies while trying to gather their older children around them so their dads could see them for that final second before the ship disappeared from view.

Eventually I just watched, without waving, for what seemed like hours, and soon I found myself standing alone. The silence that greeted my ears was broken occasionally by the wake of the ships hitting the dock upon which I stood – ships in the same convoy on their way to Guantanamo Bay. I wondered just how all of this had happened and couldn't help but wonder if, when he returned, all would be as it was.

As I drove for home, the car seemed to steer itself and I found myself at First Landing State Park–staring at the trees and imagining myself unraveling the masses of Spanish moss that clung to and appeared to engulf everything in their path. The trees seemed to be eaten alive by the moss—yet also seemed to need the moss to survive. Parasitic or symbiotic? Is there, was there a difference? Was my life—had my life turned into a mass of individual threads that, once combined, had become entangled in something that couldn't be untangled? Would the beauty and mystery of this moss be lost if untangled? Had the elegance of their combining been pre-ordained before time to create this magnificence? If not combined, what would be the resulting effect on the entire environment?

Leaving my car, I walked the park alone and sat upon a branch that had fallen to the ground—a branch covered with moss. Picking it up, I found that unraveling it broke it into shreds. It couldn't live if separated and torn apart. I smiled at the realization that some things—no matter how parasitic—simply need to be combined to live. These trees, this Spanish moss that hung from every branch, lived for each other and the mystery of their combining wasn't something to be studied or researched or fretted over—it simply was. Taking a piece of that fallen branch and the moss that covered it, I drove home alone to wait out two months.

Two months passed quickly as we busied ourselves with plans for November and December – he was due home right before Christmas. Every night I would sit alone in my room and write a letter telling him all about what lay in store for the upcoming holidays. His mom had invited me to spend Thanksgiving with them but, having never met them, I declined the invitation, telling them that I needed to be home with my family. I invited them to join my family but they, too, declined the invitation. However this was an introduction of sorts and it made Steve feel good to know that we were "communicating."

I wondered, and even laughed about, what their reaction would be when they met the girl their son had chosen. I was quite sure that I would be a shock to them. I was not his usual "type"—a fact that he had chosen to spring on them when he returned from Cuba. I was outspoken and independent and had no desire to change. Steve would simply smile and say what he always said: "You are beautiful." I would shake my un-coiffed hair, laugh at him and say, "Hope you're right!"

Soon it was Christmas Eve, and he was home. His homecoming was almost anti-climactic as we just came together so easily—it was as if he'd never been gone. He came to pick me up to attend my little sister's Christmas concert at her elementary school. When the family had gathered together, he took that "knee" of antiquity and asked me formally to be his wife—and when he slid that diamond onto my finger, I kneeled down to be with him. As I did, my hair fell into my face and I felt that now familiar hand brush my hair back—and I fell in love with that almond-eyed man all over again.

One look exchanged between unlikely bedfellows led to a life for them both.

CHAPTER 2:
THE FIRST AND THE LAST

Standing in front of the full-length mirror in my parents' bedroom, with my mom spritzing my hair until it literally froze in place, I could do nothing but smile. When brides describe their wedding day as "beautiful" and "everything I had ever hoped for," they're often talking about the setting, the flowers, the outfits, the party. But I didn't think about the "beauty" of that one day at all. I simply smiled at the thought of how much I loved that man and how—whatever I looked like—he would tell me I was "beautiful" and that the day was everything he had ever dreamed of for *us*. Finery and fixings be damned—he just wanted me and I—him!

Gazing into the mirror, watching as my mom fussed over me, and seeing my sisters roll their eyes and cough from the fumes that had sucked all the oxygen out of the room, elicited laughter from deep inside each of us – big belly laughs. It was such a release; for the past week we'd been holding our collective breath—running around, scrambling in different directions to get everything done. At that moment I realized that we'd pulled it off. We *all* realized it—and we all collapsed onto the floor laughing and talking and crying tears of "Thank you God—we did it!"

"A June wedding in Virginia would be perfect," I'd told everyone. June was "the" month for weddings, so I busily set out making appointments and arrangements and doing all those things that young brides think are so all-important. I would be the perfect bride on the perfect day in the perfect month. Book the church—check! Book the reception hall—check! Find the perfect dress—check! Make all appointments for the alterations—check! Get the invitations—check! Choose the flowers—check! Get the DJ and the photographer—check! We were on a roll—but so was the new promotion and position that Steve received.

It was mid-February—cold and dreary—when Steve received transfer orders. We had three weeks until he was to report to a new duty station at Great Lakes Naval Training Station near Chicago, Illinois. Three weeks. I had three weeks to do—what? My dad answered that question with one simple word that we all understood: "Punt." Just drop back and punt!

And punt we did! Exactly one week after we received those orders, we were married. The Chapel in the Woods was a spectacularly beautiful little place tucked away on the Naval Air Station in Norfolk—and just happened to be available. I wore my older sister's wedding gown, which seemed to be made for me and— as our parents stood up for us as witnesses and my sisters stood round us—we promised to love and cherish each other for the rest of our lives. The first pew held an aunt and a cousin or two and just a few close friends—it was the single most loving, gentle and amazing moment in my life. No invitations or flowing gown, no flowers from the fancy florist, no photographer except my dad with a Canon that he loved, no fanfare or trumpets—just my love and I realizing that we were all each other really needed. Quiet, gentle, and joyful would be the choice of words for that moment in time. Perfect just as it was—as it should have been—as it was meant to be.

Our "reception" was held in my parents' dining room with a cake that initially read "Happy Birthday" until my mom skillfully scraped the red and blue writing from its face and added sickly sweet candies that spelled out "Congratulations." My dad had mastered the art of Hawaiian Punch turned limeade and, when taken as a whole—we were a sight to behold! Laughter and pure joy punctuated the night as we ate what turned out to be, quite simply, the yummiest cake when washed down with Hawaiian limeade punch! Our wedding night was spent whiling the hours away with my mom and dad—talking about life in particular and everything in general.

As I sat there drinking in the joy of this night, I couldn't help but feel nostalgic as I watched and listened to my parents trying so very hard to not give in to the sadness that played with and teased the corners of their eyes and then betrayed them when a quiver would shake their bottom lip for just one second. The undercurrent of my leaving them was enough to drown everyone in the room and I had no life jacket to throw to them—or to me. So we laughed and talked and ate our way out of the pain that we all felt about the upcoming separation. But every now and then, my eyes would lock with my dad's or my mom's, and I could see my childhood reflected in the pools of tears that welled just beneath the surface of their laughing eyes.

The next week found us packing all our worldly belongings—which were few—into a spanking new burgundy Nova Super Sport with a ridiculously revved up engine, compliments of his Navy buddies who were part of the pack that had invaded the Kings Head Inn on that fateful night. Leaving home for the first time was both sad and exhilarating and I ached as I saw my dad cry and my mom disappear inside the house so she wouldn't see us drive away. I hadn't expected our departure to be as difficult as it was and, as we pulled out, I spied my little sister hiding in the bushes in front of the house—wiping her eyes as she started to run down the driveway to kiss us goodbye.

Seeing her run toward us, my thoughts drifted back to a time when I would run after my parents as they left for the evening. I would glare at every babysitter and envision her as the nemesis I knew she would be for the next few hours till my parents' return. I always hated to see them leave—and I would accuse them of "abandoning" us. Now, at this moment, I felt as if I was abandoning them—not starting a new life with my new husband. But, as sad as I was, I was also looking forward to a new adventure and had nothing but the highest of hopes for our future. I looked forward to us making a home of our own.

I had finished my first year of college and had decided to transfer to a university in Chicago, so we searched for a home that would allow for an easy commute for both of us. But before we began our search in earnest, we were invited to stay with an uncle of Steve's who happened to live in the heart of Chicago. We soon discovered that Chicago was a world apart from where we came from—exciting, raw, dangerous, packed with people, places, and things that pulled you and pushed you to change your life and jump-start you out of whatever comfort zone you had succumbed to in another incarnation of life. In one "New York minute"—or should I say in "one Chicago second," school took a backseat as I planned out visits and adventures that needed to be experienced. Staying in Chicago with Uncle Pat changed who I was—from a naïve student walking the marble halls of some staid university to a seasoned Chicagoan who could hail a cab with the best of 'em! It was as exhilarating an adventure as anyone could ever hope for and much more educational than what any university's famed professors could ever offer.

But soon, the commute to Steve's new position became too cumbersome and tiresome so we tried mass transit. We soon realized that mass transit was not an option, and the complete sticker shock of housing prices in the heart of Chicago was so numbing, we finally had to accept the fact that we were going to become suburbanites. Expanding our horizons and looking closer to Steve's work became an adventure all its own! Housing in Chicago and its suburbs was entirely different from the conservative Colonial with landscaped lawn and ornamental statues of the South.

But I fell in love with a little place in a city named Waukegan. It wasn't exactly an apartment; more like the upstairs three rooms of an old house that the owner was renting out "as" an apartment. We were separated from the downstairs tenants by only a thin piece of plywood that had been nailed up along the hallway stairs. I didn't mind that the bedroom looked more like a converted walk-in closet and the bathroom door was merely a curtain strung across a wobbly rod in the kitchen! The kitchen was a masterpiece in and of itself! Not having any idea just what this room was before the owner converted it into a kitchen didn't matter one single bit. It was huge and the refrigerator—I had never seen such a refrigerator. Steve said it had to be about a hundred years old but all I saw was my first fridge! The oven, while small (well, tiny actually), wouldn't accommodate any sized pan that I knew of but since I didn't or couldn't cook much—I envisioned takeout every night! That place was simply magical—it was a partially furnished three room wonder and I was absolutely certain I could find "accents" that matched the orange naugahyde couch and chair that adorned the bedroom-turned-living room décor. When Uncle Pat came to "inspect" our new home, he tried, albeit unsuccessfully, to hide his astonishment—but what he saw as "please come back home," I saw as "welcome home."

Moving day was uneventful as we unloaded our few boxes of belongings into our new home and hung the curtains we had found at a secondhand store in Chicago. And I was correct—I did find "accents" to match that orange Naugahyde furniture. The sales lady commented at the time, "I bet these are the only ones in existence." She was probably right!

Steve's commute from our new place was no longer a tiresome journey and we found that we did have more time together—time we spent exploring our new sur- roundings. Waukegan was a beautiful city and we spent a great deal of afternoon time at the local parks. At night, we would search the skyline to identify the stars and constellations.

I had always loved water—whether an ocean, lake, river or stream—it mattered not. So, when I discovered that my new hometown was situated on the shores of Lake Michigan, it quickly became my favorite place to go while Steve was at work; I'd just sit quietly by myself and dream about the life we were building. It was good, just plain good—I was overjoyed and overwhelmed by the love I had found and the life I had been given. Every day was met with excitement and we played at life as if we had no responsibilities at all except those we acknowledged toward each other.

All that changed with one phone call. Pregnant. The man on the other end of the phone said "pregnant." Having never considered the possibility of my being pregnant, I was stunned into silence. Shaking uncon- trollably, I just wept and laughed and, when I hung up the phone, I realized that what I was feeling was pure unvarnished joy! Reaching down to touch my abdomen, I marveled at the wonder of it all. Sitting at the top of stairs, waiting for Steve to return home from work, I created a mental picture of my child and pinned the hopes of the world on the shoulders of this little being that, I imagined, was weeping and laughing right along with me! The secreted existence of this tiny life, now known to me, was cause for a joy previously unknown or even imagined!

Every flutter I felt in my belly I attributed to my child saying, "Here I am! Glad to meet ya!" This child, conceived with such love and passion, would be no ordinary child—the thought of it made me laugh out loud while I waited for the return of the daddy-to-be. When he arrived home and saw me sitting on the stairs, he climbed halfway up, frowned, and quizzically asked, "What?" I stood, put my hand on my abdomen, and smiled. His eyes widened and the plywood partition he was leaning on gave way, sending him tumbling down the stairs and into the foyer below. Gathering himself into an upright position, he ran back up the stairs, two at a time, and reached for me: "Tell me—tell me everything!"

But our happiness was short-lived. I knew little to nothing about pregnancy and, having no support system in place, I felt completely alone. And I was sick. Very sick. Morning sickness was such a misnomer because this sickness was a 24-hour ordeal. And I was in pain. A great deal of pain. Running to and then fleeing from the physician's office on a weekly basis was a world apart from our walks on the shore and our nightly search of the heavens. But as my belly grew, I would tell my child that everything was as it should be and not to worry. Talking to "my little one" became my pastime of choice and we planned our lives together one day at a time.

As the months went by and I became increasingly ill, my physicians would pull Steve aside and whisper to him about their "concern" for my welfare. Losing so much weight wasn't good for me or for our child but eating had become an impossibility. Except for chocolate—chocolate would "stay down." Although this seemed strange to the physicians caring for me, it didn't seem strange to me at all. I would tell them, "Chocolate is a gift from the gods. It is manna from heaven."

But as the vomiting continued and the pain increased, I was hospitalized over and over again. Still, I would talk to my little one and assure him/her that everything was all right and that I would never let anything separate us. My prayers were always, "Please God...hear me...make this right."

Convincing myself that there was some sort of "safety" in the hospital and that, while there, the keen eyes of medical personnel would and could stop anything that even smacked of being "bad" or "wrong," I gave in peacefully to the constant "you have to be admitted." The anxiety of being sent home, alone, coupled with the continued uncontrollable sickness, became too much to handle—so Steve sent for the one person he thought could handle all this: my mom. When she arrived, she did, indeed, know how to handle this. She took me in her arms, and I rested there, surrounded and embraced by a mother's love, which was exactly the same thing I was doing for the babe growing in my body. I only hoped my little one rested as peacefully in my arms as I did in my mother's.

Day after day, I prayed. Week after week, I prayed and waited. Month after month, I prayed and waited and counted the number of days and weeks before my child would be safe if my body simply gave out. Twenty-one weeks—three more weeks till safety. Twenty-two weeks—two more weeks. Twenty-three weeks—one more week before the doctors would use their skills to save my child's life. I would rant at my physicians when they would use the word "viability" and turn my face from them as a child does when they tune out a lecturing parent. My child would survive. My child would live. Every day and every night I prayed and pleaded with God to save this child. I didn't ask for health or blessings of any other kind—just for help to carry this child for as long as I could, to keep him/her safe from harm.

As I became obsessive with the "counting," Steve and my mom would tell stories or read from my favorite books in an effort to distract me from the fear that was building in my soul. I had always loved the classics so *Pride and Prejudice* became a staple in the evening readings. And poetry—I had taken a creative writing class in my first year of college and poetry quickly became my forte—my way of communicating what I held inside my soul and in my dreams. I fell in love with rhyme and rhythm. Poetry was such a liberating form of creative writing and, whether concrete or abstract, it all made sense and touched some part of me that had previously lay untouched and unknown to the outside world. It calmed my senses and took me to a place where peace and beauty lived.

And we needed that peace and beauty at this moment in our lives. Our lives had taken such an unbelievable turn and that turn had presented us with a reality that neither of us had ever considered—life wasn't always kind or gentle. Sometimes it was quite the opposite. Thinking back to our walks in State Landing Park, I could remember the park ranger telling us to "watch out for the copperheads." We never once encountered a copperhead—we never considered the possibility that there was anything in that place of such beauty that would cause such harm. I wondered, did we just not see them because we weren't looking for them? Did we encounter them and come close to their venomous bite? Neither one of us was aware of any danger—even though we had been warned. There were no copperheads in our lives.

But being confronted with the realities of life—the ones that either break your Spirit or help you find your faith—required a strength that seemed to belong in the realm of the super human. I continued to plead with God for time and Steve and my mom continued to read the classics and assure me that "all would be as it should be." Neither did much to placate my fear or cause the obsessive worry to dissipate. And, as my prayers became more frenzied, the days seemed to pass more slowly. "Counting" became the most important conversation I had with myself and the child I carried within my body. "One more week, little one, just one more week" I would say—and wait for the movement that would tell me that the life inside my body was safe and secure.

But I couldn't get the image of the copperhead out of my mind. Where there was great beauty, was there also the ugliness of great danger? Recognizing the danger that existed within the confines of any one life was something I had never encountered, never given thought to, never fully appreciated as something real.

Recognizing it now, fully appreciating it now, avoiding that "bite" now—

Only God could help me … I had no other.

He was my first and last hope …

Chapter 3:
Meeting Death ...
on His Terms

"Some feelings sink so deep into the heart that only loneliness can help you find them again. Some feelings are so sad that only your Soul can do the crying for them."

—*Plato*

Racing through the streets of Waukegan, Illinois, I heard my mother say, "Run the lights. Hurry." I could feel the strength that coursed through her body as she held tightly to me in some sort of Herculean effort to comfort me, even though I had something for which there was no comfort.

"Hurry," she said again—almost as a whisper—"hurry."

The next thing I remember was hearing voices, voices I did not know, and I found myself counting flickering lights as I was whisked down a long cold corridor.

I wondered why no one had changed the light bulbs; it seemed so obvious to me that it needed to be done. *Why hadn't anyone else thought about that?*

I could hear my mother and Steve speaking to me and to someone else, but I didn't even try to understand what they were saying; all my attention was on the flickering.

I remember closing my eyes and realizing that someone I didn't know was telling me to "just hold on." His voice was calm and gentle, and the touch of his hand on my face felt warm and oddly comforting. I wasn't completely aware of my surroundings, and my mind wasn't capable of questioning what was happening. It seemed as if I was floating somewhere ...

As we reached the end of the hallway, I was pushed through a set of doors and found myself in an ugly green, cold room—Steve and my mother were not allowed in. The shock of finding myself alone was matched only by the searing pain that emanated from somewhere deep within my body. This realization came as a force so strong that it ripped open my very being, and I screamed. I screamed because I knew what was happening. I screamed because I was alone. I screamed because terror had been born inside of me. I screamed because I felt my child slip from my body months too soon. I screamed because I knew the beginning and the end of that moment were one and the same. I screamed because my child wasn't screaming. I screamed because it was all that I was and all that I had.

I remember looking up and seeing a nurse I hadn't realized was there with me. Tears were falling silently down her cheeks as she bent close to my face and whispered, "Your daughter, my dear," and carefully and lovingly placed a tiny bundle, wrapped in yellow, into my arms. I felt my child breathing, or at least I imagined I did, and I held onto her with some power that so was instinctive I could not name it. We stayed that way for, how long? Minutes— hours? In that place between life and death—that place where decisions are made about whether to stay or go—we were breathing together. Whether it was she who breathed for me or I for her—I simply could not distinguish. We were one. I was holding onto her for dear life and praying that she decided, that God decided, to let her stay. I felt tears spring from somewhere deep inside me—a place I had no knowledge of, a place I had never visited before.

I kissed her small face a million and one times, and then once more just so she would know something that I could not find the words to express. The pain I felt was matched only by the love I felt for this child, this beautiful babe in my arms, who was bone of my very bone and soul of my very soul.

My physical and emotional pain were so intermingled that I could not separate them, and it was in that moment that I realized they were exactly the same thing. Pain borne of torment, whether physical or emotional, are equally destructive of Spirit. I couldn't grasp what was going on in my body or soul; all I could do was fixate on her and try to pray to a God who I felt had deserted me and left me with no recourse or path to Him.

But even as I prayed, the decision was made and I felt her breathe her last. Then, in less than a "twinkling of an eye," I felt her life slip away just as quietly as she had slipped into my life. It was as a whisper. A whisper so loud—so ferocious—it was Soul-shattering. I had her for an instant in time; it was in less than an instant that she left.

The same nurse then came to me to take her from my arms. I refused to let go. The nurse paused and smiled at me—such sadness, such compassion filled her eyes. I cried – for her, for me, and for my baby girl—now so still, wrapped all in yellow.

I despised yellow.

At that point in time, all I felt was an emptiness so vast that it echoed inside of me, and I waited for my heart to stop beating. But instead, I heard the voice and felt the touch, once again, of that gentle presence who'd comforted me in the hallway, the place where I'd started my journey into darkness. I remember thinking that all the flickering lights had prophesized the end of light as I knew it. He spoke to me from under a masked face and his voice was soft and slow. As I looked up at him, I saw that his eyes betrayed his concern and I felt his tears drop onto my face. "It's all going to be okay now, I'm going to take away the pain," he said. A cold sensation assaulted my veins and I began to drift down into the blackness of a drug-induced sleep. I felt my child being lifted away, out of my arms.

I was slipping into the blackness, going deeper and deeper; but before I became one with it, I needed to say her name. A name that was mine and mine alone. I said it out loud so she could hear. I knew she would hear. I spoke just one word.

Stephanie.

Stephanie. The first word, the first thought in my brain when I awakened the next day was of her, and I felt the emptiness of her throughout my entire being. My husband and mother were sitting at my bedside but I didn't want to talk or listen or think or even be alive. I just kept my eyes closed and pretended. I pretended that none of it had happened, that none of it was real, that fear and terror were not part of my life, that death still didn't know my name. Somehow I willed myself back into the darkness – the escape—of sleep. I gladly existed there—I went there hoping to die.

In the days that followed, I remained in the hospital and "held court" for all the friends and co-workers who came by to say something they hoped would help. I remembered wondering how long they had planned their speech, how many times they'd changed the words before they realized that there were no words to soothe any part of me. They would smile, some would cry, but they all had that same look on their face. Was it pity? Or fear? Or both?

As much as I despised being in that place, I felt nothing but dread for the day I would be discharged to return to our apartment, which I could no longer think of as "home." The day came, and my mother and husband busied themselves with getting me as comfortable as possible for the ride. As we readied ourselves to leave, we didn't speak. There were no words that could be spoken without gasping for air. I remember waiting for the discharge papers, not realizing that there would be other papers to sign before I left. I was handed a folder full of "discharge instructions" advising me when to see the doctor, what number to call if I experienced "these or those" symptoms—all the usual paperwork—which I merely glanced over and initialed. When the nurses asked me if I understood what I'd just initialed, I shook my head "yes."

Then there were three other forms that required a full signature. One read "Birth Certificate." One read "Death Certificate." One read "Disposition of Remains." All had the same date. I signed.

Looking down at the pen in my hand, I noticed just how much the gold point seemed to glow against the long black casing that covered the ink compartment. As my hand began to shake uncontrollably, my husband reached for me to still the tide that was rising in my soul. But nothing humanly possible could quiet the rage that filled my heart. With every bit of strength in my body, I grabbed the ends of that pen and broke it in two, then hurled the two halves across the room and watched as they shattered into tiny pieces of black and gold. The black ink splat left on the white wall seemed the perfect epitaph; it reflected the same blackness that had now become my way of being in the world.

In the wake of Stephanie's death I felt disconnected to God and to everyone else. There was no union with anyone. No one in my life—not my husband, my parents, sisters, friends, pastors—was powerful enough to steer me away from my intended goal of self-destruction and aloneness.

Through all of this, I became a master of pretense in order to convince others that I was "recovering." I would laugh and smile on cue, say all the right things at all the right times. So others thought I was "fine," and, eventually, I got exactly what I needed—to be left alone in my self-imposed prison.

I had a newfound love of darkness that I carried with me always. Not as an anchor but as a new way of living in a world that I had come to know was cruel and unforgiving and God-less.

I thought my life's events set me apart from others and found ideas that I thought supported that notion. I read about St. John of the Cross, a 16th century saint and mystic who wrote about pain and hardship in the poem *Dark Night of the Soul.* I quoted him so many times as if I thoroughly understood what he was saying, not realizing that in reality, I had no idea. I felt so self-righteous, as if to say, "Look at me, I know exactly what St. John meant. I have suffered, I have lost, I am special." I wallowed in my "specialness" and became a Spiritual recluse. I almost destroyed my whole life in the process.

What I missed in St. John's teachings was his focus on the essentials of life—the reawakening of the Soul in our union with God; the true nature of our very being. I didn't comprehend these lessons until much later, when I found myself in the presence of a God that I thought had deserted me and left me for dead. It was only then that I could understand the pure simplicity of the magic my Stephanie had brought to me.

Her magic lay in life's greatest lesson – that the love you receive is the most magnificent expression of God's love. She chose me to spend her precious little life with, loving and being loved. This splendid little person came to this earth for such a short time—to be held and loved by me! She shared life and death with me, made her place in eternity with me—just imagine if you can. It stops my heart when I consider all she brought to me. Consider—a Soul choosing *you* to learn from and learn with, to teach and to be taught, to hold and to be held for less than one instant. She taught me about love and loss, about life and death, about giving and taking and the true meaning of our lives here. I learned more about love in those few hours than I'd learned in my entire life—the purity and simplicity, the majesty of it all—that she wanted nothing more than just to be with me!

But at the time, I didn't have that knowledge or perspective. Meeting death—on His terms—was something I was never prepared to do. I had no reserves to fight the pain and despair, no wherewithal to understand it, and nothing to guide me through it. When I realized that I did not know God, and thought that He did not know me, I went into a tailspin that threatened to end all I'd ever believed about life. Indeed, it *did* end most of what I'd been taught to believe about the goodness of a loving God.

On the day we buried our Stephanie, I wasn't breathing for myself, or standing on my own volition. I wasn't thinking, or feeling, or talking, or crying or praying. I just was. As people walked up to the grave site, Steve greeted them and thanked them for coming. I watched silently as everyone glanced over at me, wanting to approach me but not daring to—it seemed as if they all just instinctively knew and understood my need for aloneness. I stood in that quiet, peaceful place and just stared into space.

After everyone had left, I remained standing there by myself. I felt a bitterness in my heart that became a bile. It raced into my throat and made me vomit. My stomach lurched again and again and the bile ran free and unbidden throughout my entire being. My mind couldn't, or wouldn't, focus on anything other than the surreal nature of where I was and what had happened. I remember feeling confused, just overwhelmingly confused. The same questions ran through my brain over and over: *Why did God do this to me? To her?* There was no answer.

By then I was covered in my own vomit, but I still couldn't leave. I knew that at any moment, I would be asked to climb into the car and leave Stephanie behind. When that time came, I turned myself around and walked away from the greatest love I had ever known. And as I climbed into the car and shut the door behind me, I could feel my heart closing. I remember wondering if I was closing my heart to keep everyone out and away or if I was closing my heart to keep her in. Closing her in, walling her up inside my Soul, where the softness of her skin and the sweet smell of her could be kept safe for all time. Which one? It seemed to be both or either one. It simply did not matter. I needed it to be both.

A few weeks later, Steve received orders to transfer out of Chicago to San Diego. Departing that place of horrors seemed a relief, at times, but also filled me with dread.

The thought of leaving my daughter there in that cold and barren place seemed impossible to me. I couldn't accept that I would have to continue living while she would be in that frigid, lonely ground—alone.

But leave I did. As we pulled out of Waukegan headed for the highway, I could feel a deep, dark emotion growing inside me and filling my shattered soul. Hate had been born inside of me. I wanted someone to blame, so I blamed everyone. I hated everyone. I hated God.

But I especially hated myself.

CHAPTER 4:
THE CLIFFS OF LA JOLLA

The warmth of the San Diego sun was a welcome change from the cold barren world of Chicago that I had come to hate. I wanted nothing more than to leave the place that had embodied pain and torment for me, so our departure seemed like a ray of light in an otherwise dark existence. San Diego was filled with warmth and breezes that carried the ocean smells right to our front door. The wind brought memories of a childhood spent on the ocean in Virginia Beach, memories full of innocence and hope—playful recollections of that "before" time when life was fair and secure and fear did not exist for me.

Sitting out in the sun, alone, my body warmed and I felt guilty when my mind returned to the cold lonely grave where my child lay. I had left so much of myself there, in that place, and had done nothing to try to reclaim any of the "me" that lay with her. Somehow, I believed that leaving my soul with her would mean that we would always be together, always be a part of each other, always be bound as we were in those few moments of life we had together. The sun there was strong, but it couldn't penetrate the layers of ice that had replaced my once full and hopeful heart. So I sat there, outside our door, day after day, content in my "aloneness," never speaking to or acknowledging anyone who would come by and smile or try to start a conversation. And I never, ever spent time around children of any age. I made absolutely certain our apartment complex was for adults only. I couldn't face hearing the laughter of children.

Shortly after we arrived, Steve checked into his duty station and was gone most days. I was alone by choice and liked it that way, but sitting there day after day began to wear thin as neighbors would come sit next to me expecting a friendly response. It became difficult to keep them at bay and preserve my need for solitude, so I decided to roam the countryside. Where didn't matter. Anywhere, everywhere, hoping for nothing in particular and everything in general.

Somehow, I always ended up at the ocean. I would sit in the sand and stare out at the sea. I always loved the ocean. The sight, the sounds, the smells—everything about the sea was somehow comforting to me. It was vast and endless—and lonely. I could lose myself in the depths of its despair and hardly be noticed.

It was on one of these journeys that I happened upon La Jolla. The rugged beauty that met my first glance was something I recognized in myself. It was as if this place was just waiting for me before it would breathe again. Its breath caressed my face as soon as I stepped out of the car. If there was a God—this was the place He would live if He chose to spend His time among us. Even this was an understatement. And, somehow, I knew that I would come to be a part of all of it as it would come to be an integral part of me.

This place became my refuge, almost immediately. Day after day, I would sit overlooking the Cliffs. I'd arrive as early as possible and stay until the light faded, the surfers went home, the seals slept, and the birds ceased their singing. The daytime sun played with my mind, surprising me with hues that only a heaven, if one did indeed exist, could conjure into existence. The things I involved myself with—watching the surfers tame the waves, gazing out at the sea and listening to its cries, exploring the caves that had been in existence since before time—brought me some strange sense of solace.

Traversing the steps down to the caves made my heart quicken and brought tears to my eyes when I heard the laughter of children playing there; I longed to play there too. Their giggles cut through me and left gouges in my already shredded soul. I found myself both looking forward to and dreading the sounds of life that only a child's laughter can bring. I despised them for infringing upon and not respecting the boundaries I had set for myself while on this journey into the underbelly of my cliffs—as if all of it belonged to me. Yet, at the same time, I couldn't take my eyes off them as they explored as only children can. Everything was new and wondrous. Everything was a "first" and elicited squeals of joy. I secretly hoped no one recognized the same wonderment in my eyes that I knew was reflected in theirs. So I kept my eyes shielded from anyone who would smile at me or try to connect with me in any way.

My lonely heart wept for what I knew was an impossibility—to share this with my Stephanie. So I watched, every day, from vantage points of my choosing—always being careful to protect and preserve my self-imposed aloneness and, eventually, I would find myself alone in the literal sense, able to explore and become one with the cliffs I sought to own.

There were times, however, when I didn't go down to the cliffs; all I wanted or needed was to sit silently and stare out at the sea. I eventually became one with a cracked cement bench that sat beneath a dragon tree overlooking the cliffs. It would soon come to know my touch and would seemingly wait for me day after day.

I fell in love with the dragon tree the moment I sat beneath its green and white flowers, and its fragrance assaulted my soul. I wasn't prepared to accept the fact that this tree, with its fragrance, would serve as a beacon to me and draw me to it like a bee to honey. I learned that it was an ancient tree with a story as old as humanity. It sprung from the earth when Hercules killed Landon, the 100-headed dragon who stood guard over the Garden of Hesperides. Its sap was red—the blood of the dragon lived within its branches. Landon's blood spilled over the earth and gave birth to this tree, my spiritual friend, the one who shielded me from the hot sun and the peering, curious eyes of those who happened to wander by. Sitting there for hours on end, it became so easy to imagine that this bench knew only *my* touch, and I convinced myself that I was the only one allowed to sit upon its cracked and aged surface. I wondered if my bench would see another person's touch as an intrusion into a privacy, an intimacy that should never be shared with anyone. I imagined my tree withdrawing its loving protection from anyone else in an effort to force their retreat, to make them find shade somewhere else. Did my bench and tree see these intrusions as an abomination of their—and my—Spirit? They seemed to wait for me, and I sensed their welcome as I sat there, under the branches, the three of us melded into one, each feeling the turbulence of the sea that gave us life.

And so, day after day, I would return to my tree. I'd search the sea in front of me for whales and dolphins and listen for the sounds of young life that I both yearned for and was repulsed by. I loved the pelicans and birds of all manner who would return daily, having made this paradise their own. They, like me, had claimed these cliffs. I always turned my eyes to the cliffs and the masses of native flowers and grasses that filled every nook and cranny and gave life to nesting babes. I felt such life in this place; the smell of the sea as the mist rose to my face; the sight of the sea lions' playful jockeying on the jagged boulders; the sounds of the waves as they pounded the shores below and then somersaulted back upon themselves, looking for some existential ending. "Come live again" they whispered to my soul. I reluctantly and silently wanted to comply—but I didn't know how.

I found myself at odds with all of life, except in this place of solace. This sea—it spoke to me every time it catapulted itself up and over the limits of its reach. It seemed to rage for me as it crashed on the cliffs and tore itself apart, all the while knowing that, in the next instant, it would reclaim itself and be born again with an effortless and gentle memory of itself and its purpose. It would flow back and become one again with the deep darkness that was its home, and then begin the birthing process again, one that would be repeated countless times. My very being was reflected in the raging life and death play that presented itself to me day after day. I was a part of all this—my soul and the sea were one and the same. The turbulent rise and fall of the waves mimicked my still beating heart as it flowed in synchrony with a beat set by some unseen hand.

I always hated to leave this place. It had become my very own spiritual oasis. The tree, the sea—they were my soulmates. We knew each other intimately. We played together. We prayed together—even if it was to a God that I no longer believed in. It seemed they were trying to teach me to pray again—silently, not with words, but with my very life's blood. My blood, mingled with dragon's blood, coursed through my veins in an effort to will me to live again. But as darkness fell and the night closed in, I always had to leave. I wondered what it would be like, or if it would even be allowed, for me to stay on my bench throughout the night. Listening to my sea at night, without the distractions and noises of the day—what would that bring to me? I told myself that one day, I would find out. I would stay on my bench and sleep under my tree.

But every night I found myself returning to an empty apartment. I knew it couldn't be helped and, although I missed Steve's company, I cherished my aloneness—something he took very personally. Something I simply had no words to explain became a stumbling block for us—something that could have torn us apart. But try as I would to let him in, I always seemed to retreat back into my aloneness. I knew he needed me, but I didn't want to need anyone. I didn't want to love anyone. I didn't want to be anything to anyone—I just wanted to be left alone to be one with my sea and my cliffs. We both were drowning in grief that we didn't know how to express. Any word or look that passed between us that seemed to scream "help me" would be met with inexplicable nothingness—we had nothing for each other. It was both frightening and comforting. It made no sense, but knowing we shared the same unrelenting grief was somehow comforting. And knowing that neither of us could give voice to those feelings freed us from the constant need to explain ourselves to each other. We had written our own Shakespearian tragedy and like Othello's Desdemona, we were content to live a life of quiet desperation—at least, it seemed that way. Night after night, when we would lie together in each other's arms, we would have entire conversations—never voiced out loud—always secreted away in the recesses of our minds. I would silently tell him everything—I somehow had all the right words to explain the unexplainable.

But when the morning arrived, the words were still unspoken, feelings still unshared—and we would go our separate ways. I would go back to my sea. He would head back to his mountains.

I knew, as did he, that one day we would, out of necessity, be forced to share those emotions that could not yet be tolerated in the open air between us. But each morning, as I would catch sight of my cliffs, I would feel my heart move and I would breathe again. I didn't need to voice anything in this place—to my tree or to the sea. It, too, was both frightening and comforting because it all spoke the same language, one that my spirit was struggling to understand. This place—these cliffs, the wildlife, the mass of beautiful scenes and scents—seemed to have figured it all out. Each element just seemed to understand life on a spiritual level that I had no access to—a level unknown to me. They all worked together, for the benefit of everything.

And every day, I sensed that "they" were trying to teach me, to tell me, to give me something that I didn't even know I'd lost! Belonging to all this was terrifying but I knew that the answers to the questions I hadn't even asked yet were all to be found right here.

The questions I did have, those already formed in my mind and heart—I looked for the answers everywhere as I sat here on my cracked bench beneath the protection of my dragon tree. The nature of all this—the coming's and going's, the laughs, the cries, the pounding waves that crashed my cliffs—these spoke to the very nature of my Soul. I wondered what part of me, how much of me had been left behind in Chicago–and what was left here, in my spirit?

Was there even enough left of me to experience some sort of ethereal renewal of Soul, of Spirit?

I was afraid to even ask the question.

Chapter 5:
SERE Training

I had learned long ago not to ask questions about Steve's comings and goings, so this new assignment and this new training with the funny-sounding acronym for a name was no different. When we'd left Chicago, the only thing in my mind was something I wanted to change but couldn't—so it made no difference where we went or why we were going there. I did know we were heading for San Diego and SERE training but that meant absolutely nothing to me.

Steve had been unusually quiet at the start of our trip to San Diego—not knowing what to say had driven a monstrous spike between us and our conversations consisted of him saying, "Are you hungry?" or "Hope it doesn't rain," and me either shrugging my shoulders or not responding at all. We'd decided to drive to the west coast instead of flying, hoping that somehow, the alone time would help us reconnect and share what was undeniably un-shareable. Staring out the window for hours on end, I had, however, listened to Steve when he felt the need to talk. He was afraid we were losing each other—what he didn't realize was the fact that I was already lost, trapped in a maze that had no way out. I was alone with nothing but blind anger and unbridled bitterness for guides. But he made it quite clear that no matter how quiet or distant I was, he was not giving in or giving up on us. So, while on some days he didn't say much at all, on others, he talked, and continued to talk, as we traveled down the highways. And even though he appeared to be talking to himself—he knew I was listening.

And listening I was. I learned about SERE from his ramblings and wasn't surprised at what I learned. The fact that this meant more pain and anguish was par for the course these days, and I didn't expect anything less from a now tainted and ugly world. And, contrary to my opinion that SERE was a funny name for military train-ing, I learned there was certainly nothing funny about that acronym. It stood for Survival, Evasion, Resistance and Escape. He was going to war. That very same war my college friends had vigorously protested against and I had hoped would never invade my life—had just invaded our life. SERE was all about staying alive. The one question of the final exam—how to stay alive—was the one question that couldn't be answered incorrectly. It wasn't multiple choice or short answer or essay—it was to be answered in blood, with guts and raw instinct. And with the help of the tools received in SERE training, survival would become possible if captured in that far-off land of violence and death.

When we finally arrived in San Diego and settled into our apartment, I knew he would need my help in ways that, at that moment, I couldn't possibly fathom. Finding some sense of solace in what would become my daily trips to La Jolla helped me help him. Steve would leave very early each morning to head to his desert mountains and I would be left to run to my sea. I hated to admit that I never gave much thought to his training while the sea beckoned me to search its depths for life, but while there, my need for the sea was stronger than my need to know—and see—exactly what was happening in his life. My strength came from my place in the sun—it gave me the energy to help him each night as he would return dirty and tired, exhausted both emotionally and physically. We had tried to reconnect with each other but, in our unshared and somewhat unrealized grief, it had proved difficult. Therefore the opportunity to comfort him in his exhaustion was welcome; it helped me find a way to connect with him as I offered up every comfort that was available in our little one-bedroom condo. Every day, I would turn on the shower, strip his filthy body of the clothes that smelled like something from a trash heap, and wash off the grime and grit that covered his entire being. Food had become an option that he turned down until late at night—his fatigue was overwhelming and eating took energy that he didn't seem to possess.

In the wee hours of the morning, he would awaken and we would lie together—silently at first, then gradually talking and just being together. Eventually, as happens in that time right before twilight, our conversations would turn to his training and I learned all I ever wanted to know about SERE. Words spilled from his mouth that made me close my eyes and wish I were deaf—words like danger, behind enemy lines, survival, camouflage, resistance, life-saving aid, evading, and "highly likely to be captured." SERE was a life-and-death performance and the rehearsal was as dangerous as the play itself; the actors as dangerous as the subjects the play was based upon.

He was to be a military advisor out in "country"—alone, behind enemy lines, with no one but foreign soldiers to guide him and protect him as he searched for the enemy positions and reported back to someone who was closeted in an air-conditioned and comfortable hotel-turned-military base. Daggers in my heart—all of it. The word "war" took up residence in my mind. I was at war with God, with life, and with myself.

But every day, as he would leave for his mountains, learning how to survive if captured, learning how to evade other human beings intent on taking his life, I would leave to sit under my tree and search the sea in front of me for signs of life, life that had renewed itself in those same twilight hours that had gouged away more of my soul.

The thought of him going to war was horrifying, but that wasn't all. I sensed that something was terribly wrong with Steve. He was tired—too tired. He was weak—too weak. Just looking at him, holding him, told me that something was "off"—a feeling I had come to know intimately over the last year. He was losing weight from the exhaustive training—yes—but too much weight. His eyes were sunken—yes—but too sunken. He would smile—yes—but his smile betrayed something that he wouldn't share with me. Every day brought him closer to the day when he would be gone for two straight weeks, a fact that left me shaken and frightened for him. When that day arrived, I was shaken to my core as I was reminded of a hallway full of flickering lights that brought death and rage into my life.

Knowing that his first week would be filled with psychological and physical testing gave me hope that someone would see what I saw. He most certainly wouldn't say a word; he was a proud man—full of "piss and vinegar," as his dad would say. I remember the first time I actually heard that phrase. A professor speaking on John Steinbeck's novel *Dubious Battle* (1936) is said to have coined that phrase to mean full of youthful energy and raring to go after anything! Steinbeck wrote of those guys: "full of piss and vinegar who would skin you alive" if you messed with them! It was Steve's natural state of being and he would never consider shirking his duty in any way. Having no recourse, I, once again, tried prayer. But knowing that, if a God even existed, he had no reason to listen to me—I returned to my sea for comfort and solace and could only hope for the best.

When he left for those two weeks, I left for my sea. We were both fighting battles—different but the same. Physical, psychological, soulful battles that have been fought millions of times by millions of souls struggling for the answers to the very same questions that have been asked since the birth of the universe. I fought my demons on my bench under the protection of my dragon tree—he fought his battles somewhere I could not go. I seemed to have created a space deep inside me, a well of sorts that opened up to beckon and eagerly swallow any and all emotions that had a black center. I hid them away—distant and silent—in that well where no light or hope ever dared enter. My fears for Steve fit well there, so I hid them away and refused to set them free. I wondered if he had a well that was as deep and dark as mine.

Two weeks seemed like an eternity. There had been no communication of any kind and I wasn't exactly certain of the time or day that he would return from those desert mountains where barbed wire held him captive and silent. The day he was due back, there was no sign of him; when he finally did return a couple days later, I cried as I swept him into my arms. His eyes, usually bright and dancing with anticipation, were now dark and silent. His skin was yellowed and dry, bruised and drawn tightly over a frame that had lost too much weight. His lips, painful and bleeding, were thin and too painful to kiss.

I remember reaching for him and his voice cracked with emotion as he spoke, "I'm out, honey." I knew that meant he was home to stay. He wouldn't be able to do his job "over there" and, if captured, he would have most assuredly died. There would be no war for him in some faraway land. I asked no questions of him.

I needed no answers. I simply needed to somehow take this from him and give him whatever comfort I could manage to muster. He said not one word as I peeled off his clothes and helped him into a warm bath, where I gently stroked his body and waited silently for him to speak. Sometimes silence speaks volumes – this was one of those times. We both knew that words were unnecessary. It has been said, "the eyes are the windows to the soul." His eyes were closed.

He lay there in that warm water until the chill of the evening stole the warmth from the water. Sleep came quickly that night. I lay next to him and listened to the sounds of a man who was weary with life, weary of living with pain, weary of living with grief. Spiritually exhausted, he opened his eyes and smiled up at me before he closed them again in an effort to hide the tears that were forming beneath the smile. But in that instant, I could see the love still reflected in them—the same love I had seen so many times before—only this time the reflection seemed to be begging me to still love him. Laying my head on his shoulder, I assured him that he was safely home—with me—and, as he fell into what would be a dreamless sleep, I lifted my head from his shoulder, crawled out from under the blanket and sat alone, in the rocking chair that had been a "bonus" piece of furniture when we moved in. I chuckled silently as I sat in that cushion-less chair, realizing that it had never rocked anyone or comforted any living soul. It did, however, serve as a clothes hanger for travelers weary of the road and in need of someplace to throw the struggles of the day. No comfort—just utility and wood.

Throwing the dirty clothes to the floor, I sat in that chair in silence as I stared at the man who loved me from the first time he laid eyes on me and I wondered just why our world had been split open so violently. Hope had died when our Stephanie died and now this man was begging me for the love that I had promised him would last for the rest of our lives. Putting it all back together was something that had to be done—somehow. I wanted to wake him and love him but feared all I would accomplish would be waking an already defeated soul who needed sleep more then he needed me. Eventually, my back began to ache so I rose from that chair and headed off to the kitchen. I had baked a chocolate cream pie using his mom's recipe earlier that day and was in dire need of that chocolate. I cut myself an enormous piece and headed back to the bedroom to ensconce myself, once again, in that cushion-less, comfortless chair.

His breathing was shallow but regular and he was unsettled and crying out in his sleep. My heart ached for him as I came to the full realization that I was part of his suffering. He had tried to save me, to save our child, to save our marriage—at the same time he was fighting his own demons and for his own life. Had my selfishness contributed to his physical and spiritual downfall? The very thought of that had me stuffing chocolate cream pie into my mouth by the spoonful.

Feeling the need to close my eyes for just one minute was the unwanted result of too much sugar. The feeling passed quickly and I realized that I was wide awake, operating on nothing but pure adrenaline. Once again, the twilight hours arrived with new insights and accusations of guilt. Is it truth what we tell ourselves in those hours before the dawn or is it hysteria and fear? Could it be clarity on a scale unknown in the light of day when the conscious mind allows for the hidden monsters to remain hidden? What lessons are inherent in those moments of clarity, when the abyss opens fully to swallow you whole?

The sole lesson I trusted was one that had been learned at the expense of everything I considered to be truth. The only truth—the one that had been deeply carved into my Soul—was that contempt lived in truth. There was no endearing element at all. Truth can never be defined or proved conclusively—it is perception and lives in the eye of the beholder. Most of today's truths prove to be falsehoods tomorrow. What cannot be disproved, however, is that within all truth lives pain—and contempt for those who choose to believe in a world where goodness is rewarded with Blessings and evil is punished accordingly. Hemingway once wrote, "The world tries to break everyone. Those who don't break— die." There is more truth in that statement than in any other.

Grabbing myself another piece of pie, I scarfed it down and re-positioned myself at the end of the bed. I tried to silence my mind enough to lie down beside him; sleep became impossible as my mind played truth games with me. Eventually, I had a dream while still awake: I was at the foot of some minister telling me that "Only God never changes. Only God is truth." Contempt for some invisible, suppose-ed god that held out love and hope like a worm on a hook—so tempting for the hungry, but bite at your own risk—only served to enrage an already enraged heart. Sleep wouldn't come, so I ate the whole damned pie as I wondered exactly what was to become of us. As he slept fitfully throughout the night, his now labored breathing drowned out the sounds of my sea and the cries of my dragon tree mate calling to me, "Come."

I was alone once again and fought against the need to run for my life. But there was nowhere to run. Not knowing what was next, where we would be going since he wasn't going off to war, was uppermost in my mind. I spied a folder he had carried with him when he left his mountains and SERE training, and opened it to read the current orders: "Report to Coronado within 2 days for a full physical with Dr. Williams. Debriefing to follow." It hadn't even occurred to me that the weakness that seemed to be plaguing him was something other than SERE training. A full physical was probably exactly what was needed! We would be leaving soon and he needed to be healthy enough to travel. I just hoped that wherever we were going, it wouldn't be in a war zone. I knew permanent orders would arrive soon so I started packing our few belongings and shut out the call to return to my sea.

The following morning he did, indeed, report to Coronado—and I stayed glued to his side. I watched as he undressed and saw that his now too-slender frame was racked with bruises and cuts. I ached for him as chunks of black debris were pulled from his ears— leaving his eardrums rigid and infected. I cried as the physician skillfully washed his eyes of the grit that had become trapped under his eyelids, resulting in a scratched cornea that now needed antibiotic goo spread directly on his eye. A pirate patch was required to pro- tect those beautiful almond eyes and I tried to joke with him about his being "the perfect pirate now" and how proud Papa, my granddad, would be of his "patch"— just like the one he had for most of his life. Tired and still exhausted, we returned to our condo and he, once again, fell into bed and a fitful sleep.

I knew he needed me to be with him and I knew I needed to try to repair what was left of us. Spending time together was essential and, for one moment in time, I thought of taking him to my sea and sharing with him my dragon tree and my bench. But, for some reason, I didn't. I found that I couldn't go back for fear of never leaving the place that now owned my Soul. I felt discon- nected from life everywhere else but felt the need to try to live again without and apart from the sounds and Souls of the creatures that I had come to love; the place where life beckoned and gave me purpose again. But my purpose had to be helping this man, this flesh and blood man who loved me as I had once loved him. I knew the love was still there—it was just buried among the ashes that covered everything that was my life. Pre-fire love still existed and I was determined to find it again. If not for him—for me.

So I stayed close beside him. And I lay with him—in love and in masses of tears that flowed freely from the well that closeted away all the hurts and scars that tore at me every day in an effort to free themselves, to live in the light. And, as he recovered his strength, I found that I, too, was able to smile again. I had come to believe that life was so much easier when you had nothing to believe in. But perhaps there was something to believe in—even if that something was the love I shared with this man. That was truth and that, as impermanent as life and love can be—was the thing I would live for, for now.

When our orders came through, I found that we were going home—home to Virginia. We had a full month to report, which meant we could spend time with family and friends again. It meant rest and love–and home. ...

The day we were to leave San Diego, Steve told me he wanted to make a side trip to a place someone had told him was "a place of pure majesty." It was as if my dragon tree had called to him and, as we traversed the steps down to my caves, I cried and felt as if my heart had been broken all over again. He wished to explore, so I left him to his exploring and returned to my bench under my tree to bid my life with these magical friends one final farewell. How to say goodbye to these, my closest confidantes, was something I was totally unprepared to do. They had given me the will, the purpose, to breathe every day; they had given me the sights and sounds of life again; they had tempted me, teased me, urged me to live again; they had loved me beyond measure without judgment or condemnation; they had tried to bring me back to life again and given me a reason to get up every morning instead of covering my head with a pillow and hiding in bed. They tried to teach me about the impermanence of all life and showed me the rebirthing of all things that had suffered and died. But somehow I knew this would not be a final farewell, for we would meet again—someday. I knew it—as did they. I just didn't know the circumstances under which we would find each other again.

Somehow—I knew they did.

My tearful farewell was cut short as I saw Steve walking up the steps that led to and from the caves. As he approached, I motioned for him to sit beside me–on my bench. He smiled and said, "This place is just amazing, isn't it?"

He had no idea.…

Chapter 6:
The Crocheted Heart

*Knit one, purl two, knit one, purl two, pile on the icing
and gather the crumbs. . . .*

A long time ago, my grandmother tried to teach me to
crochet but I didn't pay attention because knitting
was an "old lady's game"—wasn't it? She would tell me
stories of hours spent with friends and neighbors making quilts and blankets where, sometimes, not a word
was spoken between them. They would work silently on
the project at hand; it was a strange self-imposed solitude
found in the company of five or six other women, and
my grandmother found peace there. When each had
finished with their own part, they would piece together
all the bits, then sit back and marvel at the work of their
hands. Each design was intensely personal and was
meant to expel some personal demon that couldn't be
exorcised in any other way. Grandma told me that she,
like the others, found it easier to let her fingers express
the sorrows she held captive than to say them out loud.

Grandma once said that if I could learn to "read" the quilts and blankets, then I would be privy to the innermost secrets of each woman's Soul; what they hide from the world. Every night, when she would tuck me into the old, squeaky iron bed I slept in at her house, I would wait for her "Good night, my love," then jump out from under the covers and run my fingers over the patterns that had been so carefully sewn or crocheted together. I remember seeing flowers and hearts and small children and teardrops—but, as a child, I just thought, "How pretty." I never gave much thought to the emotional lives of the women who sewed these cloths or the meaning of the teardrops that splayed across the quilts. It was a legacy that she had tried to give to me. How I wished I'd listened—and learned.

I didn't think too much about the quilts, and I didn't closely consider the beautiful crocheted blankets Grandma and the other women made, although even as a child, I marveled at the time and talent that went into the creation of them. They were so intricately designed and so carefully and wonderfully knitted together. These blankets were molded into pieces of beauty that covered each woman's precious ones with the warmth of their love.

It seemed to be such a labor of love; a labor I never completely understood until finally, as an adult, I decided to explore the meaning behind each of these carefully created treasures.

Using one of the blankets to warm my body, I ran my fingers, once again, across the lovingly pieced-together wonders that conveyed so much of life and love and sorrow. I tried to "read" and understand what each and every design meant in an effort to unearth the private sorrows that were, and had been, on display—unseen and unrealized for so many years.

The stories my grandmother told me filled my mind as we journeyed back to the east coast from San Diego. Grandma was a farm girl and, like her mother before her, became the wife of a farmer with all the trials and heartaches that accompanied that lifestyle during the Depression era. She had no formal education to speak of and had a longing for a life that could never present itself to her in any fashion. Inside her was a reservoir of all things wished for and all things that could never be. Her heart was full of sadness and joy, memories of birth and death.

Though she hadn't learned from books, she was one of the wisest women I ever knew. She was incredibly intuitive – no matter what, she just understood. With nary a question or a spoken word, she always knew what to do or how to heal whatever was broken.

She once told me that a heart was like a well-patched quilt stitched together by caring hands that made all the broken pieces look beautiful and whole. But no matter how securely it was stitched, it could still be pierced by the needles that knitted it. And the only thing that could put it back together again was those same needles. Finding the very thing that tore you apart and staring it in the face—that's hard work! But with great pain and suffering comes growth—that's where empathy is born!

In order to know great joy, you just have to wallow in the depths of the opposite.

As a child, all of this meant nothing to me. But now, as I thought back upon her words, I could see a woman's heart so full of sorrow and a strength uncommon and unknown to those who have not known suffering. What a wonder she was! How I longed to just sit with her and listen with an open heart and, unlike in my childhood, understand and make her wisdom part of my Soul.

Like my grandmother, I had a heart that had become an archive of unshared hopes, lost dreams, and painful memories—fragments that were scattered throughout my consciousness. Unlike Grandma, I could not piece it all back together to form some treasure that would give me comfort. I did not release my "fragments" in any art form, such as crocheting or quilting—they were locked away in some deep recess of my very being. I was leaving them alone and unspoken, while they grew unabated.

My longing for my lost child and for a life that would forever remain unknown and unlived filled my heart completely—leaving no room for anything else. The truth of what I sorrowed for, grieved for, would remain hidden from my view, but my imaginings would take me into the past as well as into a future as I built an imagined life with her. The "if only's" refused to leave me as I grieved for the impossible, for something that never existed, for something that was lost before it had even begun. It was senseless and meaningless and destructive. It was my life.

I tried to imagine what my grandmother would say to me if she were sitting next to me at this moment, in this car, in this heat on this road we were traveling. Would she speak or just smile that all-knowing smile of hers? I wondered if her wisdom was innate, born of past generational knowledge, or a learned wisdom born of pain. I never asked—it didn't seem the right thing to do. Over the years, I watched as her dark brown hair turned silver and her porcelain skin became etched with time. She was always beautiful and age did nothing but perfect an already perfect visage.

When Grandma's hands became painful and twisted with arthritis and crocheting became impossible, she turned to yet another path to express her love: cooking. And cooking, like quilting and crocheting, was something my grandmother used to teach me the most important lessons of my life.

How this woman could take such an everyday chore and turn it into wisdom speaks to her love of family. Cooking was a necessity on the farm, as it was her responsibility to feed my grandfather and uncles and farmhands—and anyone else who happened to wander by at mealtime. She infused every dish with great love and served it all up with such care. Three times a day she would stand at the stove for hours on end and stir and baste and roast and taste. She made dishes of all kinds, and always a huge pot of grits at every meal. The kitchen table became the place where we all learned about life from a new perspective. There was always a story, always a lesson, always a reason for every single event in life—and it was ever present in one pot or another. I would sit with her, hour after hour, and listen to her as she told stories about life and love and cooking with her mother.

To be that child again, at the stove with her mother—impossible? No, not really. My grandmother had a way of reaching into the past and taking me there with her. I needed that now. I was looking forward to sitting with her and hearing her voice as she spoke about something that, at first glance, seemed to have absolutely nothing to do with our lives but would, eventually, prove to be the very thing needed to unearth the possibility of healing. She was a visionary and saw all things that needed mending.

But, for now, the road home was proving to be long and very hot. Traveling through the desert in July was enough to make even the most ardent traveler weary. And I was weary. I so looked forward to our eventual arrival home. I felt excessively tired and nauseous and I needed to rest. I knew as soon as I reached home I could crawl into bed, cover my body with one of my grandmother's quilts, and fall asleep in the safety of my parents' home. There's something about home, isn't there, that makes us feel secure. I felt as if nothing in my life was secure or safe anymore—so home was the best and only place I wanted to be. And I knew she would be there, with a story—meant to heal and piece me back together. I didn't know how or what path she would take, but I somehow knew she would have the answer.

And she did. After our trip was over and I went home, I started cooking with my grandmother – we cooked together there, in my parents' house, for weeks on end. What happened in the course of one of those cooking sessions was just a silly little thing, really—but the lesson within has stayed with me for all these years.

How did she teach me? The ingredients for graham cracker cake and icing were her tools—and she expertly wielded them. Those ingredients, put together as they were, became a blueprint for how to piece together all the broken parts of life.

Having never attempted to make a graham cracker cake, I was a pure novice. My grandmother had made quite a few before this one and was adept at making sure this extremely delicate batter was pushed and pulled and beaten to just the right consistency before pouring it "just so" into a perfectly buttered baking pan. No detours or shortcuts! Any deviation from the exact method would end in catastrophe and the cake would be inedible. She warned me about this continuously throughout the "mixing" stage. So I watched very carefully as she skillfully and carefully followed the requirements necessary for perfection. As long as we followed the path written out on that age-old recipe, we had nothing to worry about. We now had only to wait till the oven did its job and give us the result of our labors.

As she turned to make the icing, she smiled and handed me a spoon. Mixing the icing was quite a different experience. There was no recipe to speak of—just cups and cups of confectioners' sugar and water. We "taste-tested" the icing until it became sweet and elicited an "ah" from both of us. This took a while because each of us liked a different level of sweetening. It felt so good to laugh with this woman who was so giving of herself. She would reach out for me and, after a huge bear hug, bend over to peer into the oven and say "not quite yet." Even though the oven had a timer function, she refused to use it. She was "old school" and said she didn't trust "those timer thingies."

Eventually, the cake was done and she stuck her face into the oven, closed her eyes and lovingly smelled her handiwork. Grabbing a pot holder, she reached in and pulled out the first pan and, very carefully, placed it on a stainless rack on the kitchen counter. She then turned to get the second pan out of the oven. As she did, I noticed she hadn't picked up the potholder so I yelled for her to stop. She didn't stop. She picked up the scorching hot pan and then proceeded to drop it on the floor. The cake shattered right in front of our eyes. I gasped out loud as I waited for her reaction—a reaction that never came. She turned and simply smiled at me and said "It's all right, my love. We can piece it back together." As she reached for the potholder to pick the broken cake pieces off the floor and put them in the pan, she smiled and said, "Everything broken can be fixed somehow. Shall we give it a try?"

She handed me the pan and, as I pulled the chunks of cake out of it, she told me to make sure I got each piece and all the crumbs because we needed every single one of them to make the whole fit together. She then placed each of the broken sections on top of the perfect layer and fit them all together to make a whole cake. But how to hold it all together? She handed me a spoon and told me to "start the icing." I didn't know where to start, so she took the spoon and started icing the bottom, perfect layer. The icing went on so smoothly and evenly—the perfection of it all was astonishing! Not one crumb from the crumbled layer above fell into the icing. No faults could be seen anywhere. When she turned her attention to the broken and crumbled top layer, her eyes glistened as she spoke to me so very gently about just how to make the imperfect perfect again—even if it only "looked" perfect. "There must be a starting point" she said to me. She glued that cake together with such skill and such love—glancing at me to make sure I understood what she was doing.

When she had finished, she set down the spoon and what greeted us was simply magical. A graham cracker cake—so perfect in every respect—sat on the counter before us. Regardless of the care that had gone into the construction from the very beginning, "tragedy" had struck anyway—the "insides" had to be glued back together. But once glued, those crumbled pieces of graham cracker stood whole and complete. She had crocheted a cake, mended flour and water and eggs, and turned them into a masterpiece to be admired. Yes, it would never be as strong and perfect on the inside as it would have been if not broken and crumbled—but it was worth far more now because of the love put into the mending and re-building. It held greater beauty now not despite its flaws, but *because* of them. Using icing as the glue to hold it all together only added to the deliciousness of the cake. It was her way of taking me back to a life worth living—regardless of my brokenness. She was indeed the wisest woman I had ever known.

When she finally went back to her beloved farmhouse, I knew I would miss this woman who had come to teach me about the dignity in suffering. One day I hoped to discover her long secreted-away dreams and sufferings—the possibilities of her life and the never-realized wishes she held so tightly within her Soul. She left me with a hug and a smile, and an understanding so deeply realized that no one else seemed to understand. Had she walked in my shoes? Perhaps her empathic and loving heart had been poked and pierced by life one too many times—and she was awash in icing.

Gluing myself back together—crocheting a new life for myself—came with no directions. I knew I had to find something to give my life meaning again—something to live for, something to crochet for—something to pile the icing upon.

That something had begun to make itself known in the tiredness and nausea I experienced on the long hot trip home. I had chalked my worsening health up to the extreme heat and weariness of the road. The many sleepless nights spent in motels with lumpy beds had certainly taken its toll on both of us and it seemed as if all I really needed was a good bed and a pillow that would hold my head as it fell from exhaustion. When we finally arrived home, I slept for two straight days and when I awoke, my family dressed me with love and fed me the strength and resolve I needed to get up and get out into the world. I seemed to forget about the nausea and fatigue as I allowed myself to feel the safety of family again. But, in the middle of the night, the nausea would return and I would find myself staring into a porcelain bowl, heaving my stomach into the blue water that stared back at me.

What had started as a flutter, what I had deemed fatigue and motion sickness soon made its presence known. I was pregnant.

And my grandmother, that personification of love itself—she passed peacefully from this world just a few short weeks after she held my baby boy in her arms. She kissed his face and whispered to him a story... a story of great love.....

Knit one, purl two... knit one, purl two... and pile on the icing.

Chapter 7:
Chills, Pills, and Quacks...and A Hefty Dose of Love

He came screaming into the world—so full of life and energy, creating a renewed lust for life and a purpose beyond that which I had ever known.

It had been another extremely difficult pregnancy; at one point I was told that continuing it could cost me my very own life. What they didn't understand, however, was that this child I carried inside my body *was* my life. Without him, I would cease to exist—if not physically, then most certainly, emotionally and psychologically. There was no decision that needed to be made other than where to live during the time of my "confinement." "To bed with you" came within weeks after the pregnancy was confirmed. There would be no new duty station for us—at least, not together. I would be confined to bed for eight long months.

I moved into my parents' home in the D.C. area and Steve would drive the distance from Philadelphia back to D.C. every weekend. I always waited, somewhat impatiently, for his arrival on Friday nights and pushed away thoughts of Sunday nights when I knew he would have to leave again. I was sick and in pain most of the time but I had a compassionate and caring doctor who visited me every other day to "ensure" that this child I carried would arrive on time—and alive.

My parents and Steve were concerned for me, but the only things that mattered to me were our unborn baby and the continued illness that seemed to haunt Steve's every move. I routinely shifted the conversation from my needs to his health.

Illness undiagnosed invaded our lives and seemingly threatened to unravel it at any moment. The same mysterious "thing" that had affected him so deeply in SEER training had continued, and seeped into his every waking and sleeping moment. Without me beside him, he had postponed physician visits and had, instead, convinced himself that all his problems were stress-related. Try as I would to concentrate solely on this life inside of me, I found it increasingly difficult to push aside the fears that tugged at my heart each and every time I laid eyes on him.

The dilemma I faced was one of priorities, and the solution stood in contradiction to reality. How does one prioritize things that hold equal importance? Should the top spot go to the one that, having eluded me for so long, would shortly become a reality? Or should it go to what I already had and couldn't live without? Was there a way to give both the top spot, affixing only one gold star to give them equal importance? Should I use a scale of 1 to 10 to weigh the importance of each thing, or was it better to make a list with pluses and minuses?

My dilemma was actually quite simple to explain but impossible to live with. So I did what any self-respecting person would do—I did nothing but feel what needed to be felt at the time it needed to be dealt with. My way of dealing with joy and despair required a constant adaptation of behavior—something I was becoming quite good at!

After eight long months and one week of bedrest at my parents' house, I gave birth to our beautiful baby boy. We were enraptured by his every movement, by every sound that came out of him.

When he was barely weeks old, we were assigned to a new duty station. Though I was none too eager to leave the warmth and safety of my family, I never protested Steve's orders. It was military life, and moving was just what we did, no questions asked. I packed up the few things in our possession, wrapped up our little bundle, and we left my parents' house, bound for the next location.

In living with Steve full time again, I was able to focus more on the reality of his illness. Unable to ignore the many health concerns facing us, our lives became a continual parade of physicians and tests and medicines that all proved meaningless and did nothing to alleviate—let alone explain or cure—this sickness. The fight we faced through the medical system had turned into an arduous journey—one with which we were totally unfamiliar. Confronted at every turn by symptoms that had no explanation left us...and the physicians...clueless. The hope that each new appointment with each new physician would lead to an answer turned to frustration and all hope was dashed when every appointment would prove fruitless.

We were joyous with our boy, but that feeling was equally matched by the fear of what was happening to Steve's health. Days were spent in a heaven of sorts and nights were haunted by hellish images of death and disease. We tried to keep ourselves in a continual state of playful fantasy in order to escape the desperation and aggravation that was so much a part of this "unknown" invader. Our preoccupation with illness was hidden away in the light of day, but in the dark, it came out, and we found ourselves shifting, losing ourselves to the darkness that was more than willing to accommodate our fear. Somehow, the morning light would bring about a transition in both of us and we would crawl out from under the covers, leaving the darkness behind and finding that the richness of our fantasy life was still in play. All we needed was one small wet kiss from our son and we were able to recreate ourselves and remember our true purpose in this world as his parents.

Whatever reason we gave ourselves for this night-to-day transition didn't really matter. It wasn't exactly a complete denial of reality—it was more of a separation from a problem that would, eventually, prove itself insignificant and unworthy of our time and consideration.

After a while, we got into hospital admissions, exploratory surgeries, and constant drugs. Outside of these things, life had to continue as best as humanly possible. When our boy was awake, we never spoke of any plans or goals concerning a "recovery" from this sickness.

Raising a little boy without fear, without illness surrounding him, giving him purpose and direction, and protecting his childhood innocence from all things lurking in the reality of our lives became our goal, and we seized the opportunity with both hands and full hearts. Life for him was always filled with laughter and joy and two ever-present parents who adored and loved him more than their own lives. We made sure his little life remained untouched by what swirled around our heads; it was our first priority at all times. Life was a dichotomy of emotion that pushed and pulled itself through the fear and joy as it saw fit.

Our child was too young to even notice that Daddy was losing weight and he didn't understand the sounds of vomiting that emerged from the bathroom hour after hour and day after day. He never saw the fetal position that his father would lie in on the floor every night in an effort to escape the pain that ravaged every part of his body. He never saw his mother running to the bathroom to help his father up from the floor where he had collapsed from pure exhaustion and dehydration. He was never privy to the confusion, the turbulence, the sadness or suffering, the inconsistencies of behaviors that were on display or hidden away depending on the hour of the day. He only saw—and understood—the smiles and kisses and playtimes that, no matter what, were the business of the day.

He was protected—always.

But, even as he was protected, we continued to fight our way through the system. Months turned into years and nothing purely physical presented itself that would give up and give way so an answer could be found. At least an answer that made any sense. Illness and the fight against it became a daily battle that was only interrupted by playtime or quiet walks along some shoreline of whatever duty station we found ourselves in. To say we lived two separate and distinct lives would be an understatement. To say we accomplished this with success and aplomb would be laughable—but we had no choice but to accept what we had been given and compartmentalize life accordingly.

As the years passed and Steve's illness progressed, we each learned about anxiety, depression, denial, hope, anger and all those things that make you quake in your boots. The bright spot in each of these "life lessons" was the fact that we experienced them at different times. So we were able to help the other through the unexpected pitfalls that accompany an array of emotions that have no business in the lives of those longing for normality. Being able to handle the ever-present anxiety had become a snap—it was the fear of the unknown that caused the night sweats and the night terrors. The constant battle that was being waged in his body was also being waged in my heart. I was profoundly confused and found myself in conflict with every idea that entered my mind. With each new symptom, I was forced to alter my thinking, and my emotions never stopped teasing me. I was a mixed-up mess of anxiety, joy, fear, confusion, judgment, anger, hatred, exhaustion and just plain ole' numbness. Tragically powerful in my ability to flow from one extreme of emotion to another, I was a Master of Distraction and a self-professed Ph.D. in Chasing Dreams. I had become a stranger to myself in the light of day and hid under a rock in the darkness lest someone find me, pull me out and force me to recognize what I had become.

And what he had become. There was no denying that something was terribly wrong. But being undiagnosed left us with little power or control to navigate the waters we found ourselves drowning in. Year after year, one physician after another saying "sorry" or "I have no idea" or "let's try this or that surgery," or the ever present "It's all in your head."

And so, year after year, we survived as best we could—always searching for an answer as one question after another rose and then fell victim to "Sorry—we just don't know."

New duty stations, one after the other, always began with physician visits where I would drop a stack of medical records on the desk of some "newbie" and watch as he'd flip casually through the pile and then order the same tests previously conducted—and then dismiss us with the usual "We'll call if we need to see you again." At times like these, the anxiety would become overwhelming. There was no way to settle the mind, to find peace. I couldn't go to some remote space in my brain that would allow me to sit quietly and reflect. If I had, maybe I could've come up with a way to solve the problem that was constantly taunting us. Maybe.

But as things stood, help seemed to be non-existent and we—or at least I—had no faith in anything but my love for my boy and the man who clung to us both as if we were his very life's blood.

I was so grateful that all our assignments were for shore duty, which gave us access to physicians and hospitals at a moment's notice. His career path had changed over time and sea duty wasn't required—or at least it hadn't been necessary or assigned yet. His job, I would learn, was one that kept him behind barbed wire and fences lit up by the lights on the little shacks manned by armed guards. I wasn't even allowed in.

That all changed—and so did our lives—in one fell swoop. When the orders arrived, I felt as though someone had kicked me in the gut. He was going to sea on a Guided Missile Destroyer, and not only that, but he was going for nine months. Nine months cooped up with only a medic on board—or possibly a physician—with nothing at their disposal except a stethoscope and a thermometer for tools. I would discover that this assignment was a direct response to his new job title – "Electronic Warfare Officer"—to be exact. I had no direct knowledge of what that actually meant—but I did know that there was not one single thing that could be done to stop his leaving.

The ship departed on a warm, sunny day and I stood there, holding my little boy's hand, waving goodbye until I couldn't see Steve standing on the deck anymore. We had moved to Florida, the homeport of this destroyer, so I was determined to make the most of the sun and sea and spend the days playing in the sand with my boy. Nine long months spent worrying about something I had no control over could do nothing except make us both miserable—and that simply wasn't an option—so I told myself, "It will be ok" over and over again. I tried to make myself believe in my own thoughts, to believe in something other than fear.

It only took two months. Two months before I received a call and a visit from two uniformed officers with the "news" that Steve would be arriving home and reporting to the hospital on base for "surgery." He would be home in three days. Appointments with an internist, a gastroenterologist, and a surgeon had already been scheduled and it was their "hope" that I would gather every note, medical record, and test result that I had in my possession and deliver them that day. Needless to say, I complied—that very day.

I arrived at the hospital a few hours before Steve was expected and met with the physicians who, I hoped, would be the ones to finally have an answer for us. How very wrong I was! They, like the others, had no clue where to even start, and the fact that they were already considering surgery without ever laying eyes on him was concerning. In fact, in my opinion, it was just plain negligent and stupid! I could not allow this to happen—but what alternative, if any, was open to us? I had to find that alternative before they just started cutting on his already cut-up body.

But I needn't have concerned myself with this dilemma. There would be no surgery here, with these physicians, in this military hospital. He was just too ill and any anesthesia at all would be too risky. So, after being admitted to the hospital for a full two weeks for fluids and "tests," he was sent home.

Exactly one month to the day after he returned home, we found ourselves sitting before another uniform pushing medical discharge papers in our direction. The U.S. Navy was discharging my love because he was too ill to continue in his role—and they were too inept to discover the cause so they just sent us on our way. I was overjoyed—he was not. But I knew, deep in my heart, that this discharge would lead us to the right place, the right physician and the right diagnosis that would save his life.

We were going home—this time, to stay. There would be no more new physicians who looked at us with that blank stare. We would find the right one that would be our only one. There would be no more duty stations or moves that would take us—or him—to places where help was non-existent. I was determined to find the best civilian physician that I could find and, with help from family, we wouldn't be alone anymore. And our little boy would have family to be with, play with, and just "be" around.

Just a few short days after we arrived home, we walked into that physician's office. It hadn't been hard to find him and he saw us immediately. I had delivered every scrap of paper, every medical record in my possession to his office the previous day and it only took him ten minutes to have his nurse call us into his office immediately.

Little did we know the answer had been right in front of our noses the entire time; it lay there in plain sight. The clues we never picked up on were found to be screaming at us from his everyday life. Hidden away, hour after hour, in small, closeted rooms with radiation and "new" warfare systems—he'd been exposed to elements that no human being should ever be exposed to—and it had literally eaten him alive. Years of exposure had led to inflammation compounded over and over again—inflammation which could not be seen or proven by any medical technology available at any of the clinics where we had been sent.

As I sat there, listening to this physician describe Steve's exact symptomology—my mind replayed a conversation I'd had with one of his surgeons five years earlier. He'd told us that Steve's illness was, most likely, caused by an ulcer—a really big ulcer—and that surgery to remove part of his stomach was necessary and would "fix" the problem. I remember speaking with this surgeon shortly after he had completed his part of the procedure and, as he walked away from me, he turned and quipped, "His pancreas looked a little inflamed—but not to worry—this surgery will fix that!" I became fixated on it, this one flippant remark made years ago by a doctor whose name I couldn't even remember—if I had known it at all. I could see his white coat as he hurried through the exit doors that led out of surgical recovery. I'd stood there next to Steve, who lay asleep from the drugs meant to curb the pain of what had been done to his already ravaged body.

Right then and there, a hardened heart and a stiffened resolve became a way of being and I realized that the old hatreds and fears of the past had returned to knock us to our knees once again.

After the doctor – an internist—told us the symptomology, he finally revealed the diagnosis. Then he stopped short, explaining that it wasn't his specialty, and that he couldn't discuss "the possibilities of treatment."

The dirty work of treatment would be left to the second doctor – the oncologist. As we were ushered down the hallway to his office, I merely glanced at the name on the door and the specialty of the man we were about to meet, the man who would reveal our fate for the next several weeks, the man who would change our lives forever.

We were ushered into his plush office. After we sat in the chairs in front of his desk, my shoes fell from my feet and I buried my toes into the deep beautiful softness of the Oriental rug that adorned his floor. As he walked into the room, I noticed his eyes were soft and blue—like his carpet—and I almost laughed. As Steve reached for my hand, I turned to look at his face—a face I knew as well as I knew my own—and saw the same fear I knew was living behind my smile.

I didn't look at this physician as he started talking—I stared directly at the man who was my husband and the father of my little boy. I didn't want to hear. I felt like the puppy dog that turns his face away from his owner as he is being chastised—as if the very act of turning away would make me invisible. As if I would be unable to comply because, having declared deafness as my weapon of choice, I simply could not or would not hear the instruction ... or the truth that was my life.

Watching the jawline of the man I loved stiffen—then fall—then stiffen again as he listened to the words that I didn't want to hear, I turned my face to the man speaking and listened.

Pancreatic cancer had come home to roost.

Chapter 8:
Tinker Bell is Grounded

Sometimes it's a word. Sometimes it's an action. Sometimes it's merely time itself. But sooner or later, the fairy dust of childhood wears off and we lose our fairy wings—they become useless appendages. The fairy bell goes silent, never to be heard again in either our waking or our dreaming lives. As the innocence of youthful imaginings abandons us, we find ourselves wide awake, aghast as we confront the reality of the world in which we find ourselves embroiled. The fog of childhood lifts, real life grabs us by the hand—or the throat—and leads us into that never-never land of non-belief. The safety of our youthful naïveté is replaced with the numbing actuality of life in all its glory.

Until that innocence is stripped away, we live in a land of make-believe and wishes that could and would come true if only we "wished" hard enough. Remember what Peter Pan said? "Close your eyes and believe." That keeps Tinker Bell alive and flying loop-de-loops.

Loss of innocence doesn't always come about as a result of some horror or trauma that strips children of their childhood. "Growing up" is, oftentimes, the culprit that sneaks in and, as with the magician who shows you all the tricks of the trade—you're left sad and wishing you had locked all the doors and windows of your soul as each birthday approached. "Growing up" lurks around every corner just waiting to reach in and steal the last bits of magic that exert a protective—although unrealistic—force on anyone who has somehow managed to escape its grip for any extended period of time. Yeats described it perfectly: "The beautiful and the innocent have no enemy but time."

At the time of Steve's diagnosis, innocence had abandoned us long ago and beauty existed only in the son we adored and cherished—so time held no special significance beyond each day. It didn't hold any power over us except for the endless tick… tick… tick of the passing minutes and hours which dictated the comings and goings of our lives.

During this time I managed to, somehow, keep my fairy wings at half-mast—quite an accomplishment given Steve's ongoing illness, and yet a necessary and vitally important task. After my son was born, I needed to introduce him to a world full of joy and pretense where we would play the day away and fly unfettered as we saw fit. This make-believe world was my salvation and it was filled with as much love as humanly possible as we locked away anything that smacked of reality. Keeping that fairy bell ringing in his tiny ears was the most important task in our daily lives.

So every day I would grab the bottle of "fairy dust" we had found at Disneyland and sprinkle our heads with the tiny pieces of glitter that kept our gossamer wings from lying useless against our sides. I wondered, at times, whether our wings were spun from the finest silks or from the spider's thread, attached to a web that would prove to be deadly. If you try to maintain a sense of wonder while the spider's web closes – if you struggle – the web becomes tighter and tighter until you are engulfed, your wings pulled out at their very root.

My wings lay flat at my sides that day. Sitting in front of some stranger as he laid out detail after detail regarding this diagnosis and the upcoming challenges we would face left me numb; his words had exactly the opposite effect he had expected. I had no questions for him, nor any expectations; nothing of any value to add to the conversation. I simply stared out the window and pictured myself somewhere else. I understood him explicitly—but wanting to dis-identify with my life once again, I imagined a time and place where I could close my eyes and fly away from the reality that was right in front of my face—the reality that was now ours to live.

When my daughter died all those years ago, instead of dealing with her death in some constructive manner, I turned inward and refused to accept it. I lived in an imagined world with her and let rage and hatred rule the moments when "we" weren't together. I created my own little ocean of pretense where I could splash around with my mermaids when life threatened to impede with its ugly realities. When those realities did, indeed, find a way into that inner sanctum of pretense, I would retreat, once again, and run like hell back to the joyful numbness of my imaginings.

As this seemingly heartless physician continued his well-practiced dissertation about life and death and "timelines" surrounding chemotherapy and radiation and survival rates, I felt the life being sucked out of my very being. The reality of the world that had been swirling around my head for so many years was finally having its way with me. The concrete walls I had so carefully built around me to keep the world out, to keep the gossamer wings beating, were crumbling. In that moment, as I sat there in that office—half listening, half thinking, half breathing—the walls fell, my thoughts gave way, and, in an instant, I grew up and gave up every pretense that had kept me functioning.

Listening to the continued droning on and on of this physician left me mindless; his continued lecturing on the dos and don'ts filled my brain with an apprehension that coursed through my veins and brought me back to an earlier time when fear ruled supreme in our lives. As much as I wanted to be sitting there, next to my love, holding his hand with all my strength, I also wanted to run—right or wrong—I just wanted to run. I searched for a way to return to that secret world of my own making where everything sacred to me was protected. But as hard as I tried, I found that place no longer existed—it was no more. There was no illusion here, no pretense to be found or built, no hiding place or shelter from this storm—I could not find a way back nor could I stop the incessant ramblings of the man speaking to us of something that was wrong on every level of my thinking or believing. He was speaking to us in the cold light of day—and he was speaking about death.

Not wanting to hear or listen to the statistics that were pouring out of his mouth, my mind drifted back to a class I had participated in—an elective—spiritual in nature, that I thought would prove valuable in some strange non-spiritual way. Not having any spiritual leanings at all, I still found the subject interesting, maddening, and worthy of study. Approaching all spiritual matters from an intellectual point of view became a way to disprove, nullify and ridicule whatever I found to be "food for the masses;" I believed the unprovable was taken as truth only by the naïve.

It was a course of study that began with the book *A Course in Miracles*. The words "Nothing real can be threatened" and "Nothing unreal exists" followed by "herein lies the peace of God" elicited such a fierce response from somewhere so deep inside my Soul; I remember almost walking out of the class. Given the fact that these words were merely the introduction to the course meant that I was about to embark on a journey that surely would create waves of anger as I debated the ridiculousness of such words being presented as truth.

Sitting there in the doctor's office, the words presented in that course replaced the words assaulting my ears—and I found all of them meaningless and unbelievable. The doctor presented concepts as truth and anyone not "aware" of these concepts was not "fully awakened" yet and in need of salvation. The mere thought of that course—especially in this moment— made me want to laugh out loud.

I must admit that I did not complete the class—I left the minute the instructor read, and I quote— "Forgetting all our misconceptions, and with nothing to hold us back—we can remember God" followed by "Beyond this, learning cannot go. When we are ready, God Himself will take the final step in our return to Him." Being told that God's love was unambiguous and unalterable—it was simply a lie. Being told that Steve would die—it was a lie. Being told that "Nothing real can be threatened"—it was a lie. Steve was real and his very life was being threatened. There were no misconceptions here—this had nothing to do with something that wasn't "real."

I had many reasons not to have faith in *A Course in Miracles*. For one thing, the statement, "….God will take the first step in our return to Him" begged the question: Why on earth would I want to return to Him? And how about "Forgetting all our misconceptions…we can remember God"? The implication that my perception of God was a false interpretation of God's love was simply ridiculous. When I spoke of God, I spoke from experience. It was knowledge that I had gained from having lived life—not from imperfect perception. It was knowledge of the whims and wanderings of some "thing" out there that probably didn't even exist. And, if He did exist, then He was the responsible party to all the sufferings of the world.

Just as I abhorred the certainty inherent in *A Course in Miracles*, so I wondered if I could challenge what the doctor in that room presented as "gospel." I wanted to break it down and create our own reality, one in which the "facts" as presented to us were disputable.

What I could not do, however, was remain separate and apart from the reality that had now sucked all the oxygen out of this physician's office. The reality that the diagnosis—on the surface, at least—lined up with Steve's symptoms and history. The reality that it meant a course of treatment that would be near unbearable.

I had thought, after Stephanie died, that I had grown up and could handle whatever life threw at me. I had thought that when she left us, that my innocence had died with her—but I found that to be absolutely inaccurate. Sometimes it takes a second storm to realize that you hadn't been living in a world devoid of innocence; in fact, you didn't live in the actual world at all. Sometimes, it takes a second storm to pull you, kicking and screaming, into the world you truly belong in: a world full of tragedy buffered by hope and a realization that time can be a two-edged sword, bringing either disaster or salvation. There was no separation from this reality. Not today or tomorrow...

The world had just become real.

I knew there would be hospital stays, radiation visits, chemotherapy trials and tribulations, and tears...fountains of tears that I would never release; that would never fall from my cheeks onto his. I knew the time was here for me to step up, to be present in a way that I had never been present before. There would be no more time for childish, self-serving conjuring's or magical thinking.

Little did I know that time would run out that very day. As we left the office, we were handed a script for blood tests and directions to the radiology department at the hospital across the street.

So began the journey to save the life of the man who held my hand and smiled down at me with a resolve so ferocious I could hear his heart roaring. Having no knowledge of the effects of radiation, I could feel myself trying to imagine a scenario where "it was no big deal" and even found myself expressing that out loud. Neither one of us wanted to be "real;" neither one of us wanted to speak the truth as it had just been spoken to us; neither one of us wanted to confront what was, at its worst—unalterable, at its best—questionably hopeful.

I thought back to *A Course in Miracles* and a debate about death. Isn't it easy to speak of death as some phenomenon that never touches a life in any appreciable way? If we are truly spiritual beings and if nothing real is ever threatened, then doesn't that mean that death isn't real? That no one ever really dies? That we simply change form and exist in some altered reality? All I knew was this one thing—for me, in this here and now, Death was real. It was ugly and inflexible and final. And it terrified me—for him, for me, for our little boy.

As he dropped my hand and disappeared into the bowels of the radiation department, I was left shaken and speechless. All I could muster was a smile and a wave before my stomach lurched and I vomited into the nearest trashcan. I needn't have been embarrassed, as I heard "Been there, done that" coming from family members waiting for their own wives, husbands, and children who had disappeared down the same hall-way on their way to what was not so lovingly referred to as "the radiation chambers." "First time is always the toughest" someone said. "Nah, it gets worse—depend-ing…" rang in my ears, and my stomach lurched again as the receptionist handed me an emesis tray. Tears sprang from my soul and I found myself in the arms of a woman who looked to be my age. She was "an expert at this," she said as she held my hair back away from my face. Feeling stupid and pitiful, I realized that all these people felt the exact same way and that it was "okay" to "leave it all here—before they get back." Thankful and grateful for the help, I began to understand that radia-tion was a big deal and that I was about to discover just what I was made of.

Radiation. The chills racked his body. He shook so violently—his teeth rattled and his bones cracked. I held him so tightly I thought I would break him. Wrapping him in a blanket, then another and another in an effort to stop his unstoppable shaking, I buried my head in the softness and silence of the folds at his chest. There was nothing I could do but hold onto him and listen to his heart beat—faster and faster. "They" said, "it will pass in a few hours." "They" said, "if he is burned—use this" as they handed me a tube of ointment. "They" said, "see you next week—after his chemo." I said nothing. Neither did he. We didn't need to say a word.

The egocentricity of childhood had vanished. Unmistakable clarity and purpose had filled in every gap that existed in my mind; determination and awareness of reality had become primary fixtures. It was inconceivable to try to survive this any other way than to face it head-on with strength and resolve.

Once again, the words of *A Course in Miracles* ran through my mind…"Truth is unalterable and can be unrecognized—but never changed." Did I believe those words? Did I have a choice? Was the truth of this disease truly unalterable? Was this "truth" merely perception? Perception based on research, granted, but was there a way to change it? I was determined to make a way, to choose a way for us that would alter the truth of this disease as presented to us. Did I have to recognize this as truth or could I, could we, live in a state of "unrecognized truth" that would make it, force it to become mere perception? Was this my—our—way out of this? To deny the truth as told to us in favor of a truth that was just waiting to be discovered—was that the key to survival? Instinctively, I closed my eyes and told myself, "Believe…believe…believe"…as I listened for that damnable fairy bell.…

Saying goodbye to the fairy dust and the ringing of the fairy bell was as difficult as it was depressing. Knowing that we needed help, I reached out to the two people who had been there throughout every joy or sorrow I had ever experienced in my life—my parents. I would need them to keep the fairy bell ringing and the magic alive for my son. Handing over the most precious thing in my life—my son—was unthinkable and almost un-doable...but the choice was made when the doctor opened his mouth and the words "terminal cancer" escaped from his lips. That choice, once made, was one I had to learn to live with. It was the only choice that could have been possible.

I shifted from putting away my gossamer wings and wiping the fairy dust from my hair to holding emesis bowls and placing cool washcloths on his face after chemo treatments. Swimming with imagined mermaids and magical incantations was replaced with "It's almost over" and "I'm here, my love" and "Only a few more"...words that hung in the air and never quite connected with the reality of our world. As his condition progressed and more treatments were ordered, we were forced to move into the hospital. We became "lodgers" in a "hotel" that was populated by physicians and nurses and machines that screamed and hissed at you and dared you to retaliate. Daily showers, shampoos and clean clothes became a thing of the past as did our comfortable bed and soft sheets. White, fluffy, softened towels were replaced by dingy, industrial-strength, worn-out rough cloths that I discovered were the perfect alternative to a professional exfoliation treatment. Playtime was replaced with napping—whenever possible—and dining together became eating whatever was available whenever it was possible. Life was difficult and depressing and the days were long and lonely. We were isolated from all things loving and gracious.

But every night, at exactly nine o'clock, the phone would ring and I would answer to the sound of "Hi

Mommy." And, as my heart would break and soar at the same time, I would hear "Can I talk to Daddy?" Handing the phone to the man who answered to "Daddy" always brought tears to my eyes—which I camouflaged and fought against with a smile and a little laugh and a "Here he is, baby." Hearing Steve say, "How's my little man tonight?" was as devastating as it was reassuring. Emotions flowed and combined in some sort of mixed-up, jumbled mess of anxiety tinged with a controlled, quiet hysteria that could never be shared.

I tried to push aside the fear that one day, I would have to lie to that little boy and tell him that Daddy couldn't come to the phone right then. But that time wasn't now and that lie would just have to wait.

In the meantime, I would just listen to their conversation as his daddy would ask, "How was your day, honey?" then close his eyes and imagine the pure joy on the face of that little boy as he excitedly recounted all the adventures he had been on that day. I, too, would close my eyes and remember the days of magic and gossamer wings shining brightly—and never let a tear escape from my eyes.

It was then that I discovered something about pretense and imagination. The four most important words in any language weren't words of strength or weakness, or love or fear—or even separation or death. The four words that rang loud and clear in my mind each and every night before I lay down on the hospital cot became my mantra—"Once upon a time...." They became the most powerful words ever spoken or considered. Those words are the story of and the making of every life ever lived…

The transforming power of "Once upon a time" isn't or wasn't pure fantasy. Those words provided an opportunity to alter what was perceived as unalterable. They provided a chance to change the story, a hope for the future that would turn their "truth" on its head. "Once upon a time" would provide the miracle that was needed and, if perception was, indeed, a function of the body— then belief in that perception could become our truth. Could it not?

Where there had been softness and fragility—there was now raw strength and determination. Where there had been confusion and fear—there was now unmistakable clarity and a keen awareness of what had to be done.

I had been grounded. My wings had been clipped or perhaps, like Icarus, I had flown just a little too close to the sun… had singed my wings… and needed to learn my true limitations. In fantasy—there are no limitations.

The question that presented itself to me now—were there limitations in truth? Or could truth be just as fleeting as perception?

I needed to know.

CHAPTER 9:
BAPTIST MEMORIAL HOSPITAL

I knew every nook and cranny of this Baptist Memorial Hospital. And it knew me. In the wee hours of the morning, when Steve would finally fall asleep, I'd walk the hallways, peeking into room after room, checking in with the families of the other patients on our floor. None of us slept very well at night and, in our aloneness, we reached out to each other in hopes of drawing some sort of "line in the sand" that death wouldn't dare cross.

We learned everything we could about each other and familiarized ourselves with the patterns of everyone involved. After the first few weeks, we didn't even need to speak—our eyes spoke volumes and made words seem inadequate and unnecessary. And our smiles, as artificial as they were—were all the same smile. We just understood…we all felt the same messy emotions. Emotions for which there were no words. None of us felt the need—nor wanted—to voice the pain in our hearts. It might have been impossible to give sound to the groans of despair echoing in each of us. No one wanted to delve too deeply into the reality of our situations, preferring, instead, to navigate the world on a purely surface level. Talking about what was real would take us too close to the floodgates, the ones that were holding back the rivers of Hell.

None of us were heroes. We all had our personal fantasies and living in them kept us alive. Fantasy expelled all tragedy, all error, all fear and kept us from the truth. We stayed away from the truth at all costs, as it threatened to take any power or control we mistakenly grasped and believed was ours. Holding on to that imagined world was the ticket to escaping the facts of our existence—this was especially true at night.

The nights held little peace for anyone. Quite the contrary, the hours between midnight and 4 am were filled with dread. They became the witching hours and my time of wandering would begin in some futile effort to make sure everyone was "in place" and that everything humanly possible had been done to ensure everyone survived the night. It didn't take long for others to join me in this effort, as we'd take turns checking in on each other with a reassuring glance that was completely understood as "I am here for you" and "we're all still here." It was a small comfort and yet we all needed that little bit of Grace.

Some needed the Grace less than others; those who believed in a loving God and His Grace looked to Him for comfort. I didn't know whether to feel sorry for them or be jealous of their faith, which I now considered to be utter naiveté and an imagined escape route from the realities of this world. But, during my nightly wanderings, none of what I believed mattered. We needed to be there for each other in any way we could. Our lives had become overwhelming and anything other than what we agreed upon as our mission was meaningless.

Everyone walked on eggshells. We watched every word we said and every move we made. If anyone acted distant or spoke aggressively or angrily, it cut through us like nothing else. It was difficult trying to hold everyone together when you couldn't even hold yourself together, and yet we did it, out of a deep need – sticking together was the only thing that made sense any more. It was our own little fragile production, like being in a play—if anyone "broke character," we all fell. Fragmented, we were vulnerable. As a make-shift family—albeit one formed by fear and denial—we were strong, a force to be reckoned with (so we thought). We were a force that could alter reality.

I did know on a very basic level of knowing that this pretense of power was nothing short of absolute denial. So I wandered in search of something that would give me strength and help me recover from the insipid weakness that infused my every interaction with the world.

My nightly wanderings became obsessive, as night after night I walked the halls, peering into the adjacent rooms and hearing the sounds of sleep—something that had become foreign to me. Many a night I thought about taking some of the meds that were offered to me—meds that would help me sleep. But I never actually wanted to sleep. I had no desire to face the demons that inhabited my dreams. I convinced myself that if I slept, he would die alone, and that simply was not an option. In the madness that had become my mind's playground, I imagined I would have unlimited power and control if I just stayed the course and stayed awake; it was my own personal neighborhood watch. I knew I was running on pure adrenaline but I pushed and pulled and forced myself to remain awake. I read, watched TV, visited the nurses' station, stuffed my face with any food I could get my hands on—everything and anything. I could not afford to fall asleep. This would go on until I literally dropped onto the cot next to Steve's bed.

I soon discovered that walking was the best way to avoid giving in to my need for sleep. So, while he slept, I wandered. So as to never wander too far, I memorized the routes that would take less than five minutes to get back to the room. One of those routes took me to the kitchen, which eventually became a bright spot on those long, fearsome nights. I would come to know the early rising cooks who prepared the meals for the patients and for those of us who were known as the "cot" people— and they would come to know us as well. I always looked forward to Tuesdays, which were blueberry cobbler days, and Thursdays, when they cooked up apple crisps or biscuits, served up piping hot and delivered with a huge smile and the occasional hug. These moments provided glimpses into a normalcy not present in my world of fear and confusion.

The cooks began to look for me at night and had dishes ready for me to try. There was something about this that reminded me of home—like raiding the fridge at midnight—and it always made me sob or laugh or just explode in some sort of frenzied combination of both. Returning to my cot to sit alone with a plate of some decadent dessert balanced on my lap—I would imagine a reprieve, a waking dream that would show me the way out. I would plan and scheme and design an escape route where nothing could stop us from returning to our world outside. But then my thoughts would go to La Jolla, where I sat alone in a room, in a rocking chair, watching this same man sleep fitfully while I ate pie. It was years earlier, but I'd had the same thoughts, same fears, same sleepless nights as now. Going outside would not be an escape for us.

Here at the hospital, my stomach full of dessert, the ever present taste of bile in my mouth, the sound of his breathing would eventually bring about a hypnotic fatigue that slapped me in the face and made my eyes water from the need for sleep. How I wanted to empty my mind of this confusion and anger. How I wanted to free my body and soul of all feeling. To be numb and stupid was what I craved. I have heard it said there is no enmity in knowledge. I beg to disagree. I found only fear and brutality in knowledge—especially in the darkness.

But as long and fearful as the nights were, the mornings arrived with new and unwelcome information. Confusion always reigned supreme as we'd try to find a place in our brains that would accommodate the never-improving medical reports. Every day was simply a mirror image of the day before—medicine, more medicine, different medicine, sunken eyes, pain, fear, questions, anger, more questions that had no answer, endless vomiting and, at times, the hushed voices of the doctors and nurses as they closed the door of a patient nearby. We all knew what that closed door meant.

All day long, throughout our remote little world, the sound of sobbing, anger and grief was so intense, it could be felt by everyone in every room. There was no such thing as buried pain—it lived and thrived in the open air. We had fallen down the rabbit hole and trying to claw ourselves out was useless. We all lived in the same bubble of depression and despair and we all had the same sense that something had snuck into our lives, uninvited, and sucked all the meaning out of those things we'd built our lives on. Things we thought were so important seemed to pale in comparison to our new realities. Money, titles, degrees, ego—all meant nothing in light of the truth of our newly discovered mortality.

I vacillated between denial of the fact that we were never going to leave this place as we'd entered it— together—and anger, which filled my soul and took me back to the moment when whatever God existed had surely abandoned me. As the hours turned into days, and the days into weeks, my reaction to everyone and everything was one of anger. It became my mode of behavior. I was angry at Steve for the possibility of his leaving me. I was angry at myself for being angry with him. I was angry with the doctors who couldn't heal him. I was angry at life for inflicting this on us and I was intensely and overwhelmingly angry at a God that

I constantly denied existed but always felt the need to blame and heap profanity upon. I had long ago lost any faith in the saving Grace of some God who had seemingly targeted us for unknown reasons. He had at His disposal a weapon I had no power to defeat—time. Time was nothing to Him. But to me, it was everything. And I needed more of it.

I needed more time to make some sense of this. Nothing about this existence made any sense to me. I knew that I had to somehow prepare for the fact that the days and nights ahead would be numbered, but I had no idea how to fit this into the brick and mortar foundation that we had so carefully built since we lost Stephanie. I knew that life would become a living, waking nightmare and it would be more and more difficult to live in denial and false hope. There would be a reckoning. There would be a reckoning that would be so pervasive, it would rock the very foundation of my life – once again.

But for the time being, I was living in conflict and tension with reality, simply seducing my mind to sleep. Pure foolishness—I knew that! I knew it was putting me on the sidelines of life. And yet I couldn't stop chasing my illusions.

I was in the fog of delusion, and I felt the fear of the encroaching villain: time. Watching Steve from the vantage point of time was excruciating. Each and every hour became my enemy. I had no idea how to fight this villain. Until then, I'd never given much thought to the concept of time; it just simply *was*. But it had become everything. All the "before's," the "now's," the "then's"—my time, his time, the time left, all the wasted time, the pure illusion of "all time," the "forever's" that never actually exist for anyone, the end of all time (what and when actually is that?). It was all swirling around in my brain.

Knowing that time was a human concept, I played with the thought, or delusion, that I could somehow manage it or beat it or change it to meet my needs. I wanted to steal time, to make it mine and do whatever I wanted to do with it. I tried to convince myself that time was illusion, delusion—something I could control if I could only understand the mechanics in play. In my saner moments, I knew the impossibility of these thoughts. But in my desperation, I needed to believe that somehow, something would suddenly present itself to me and I would then be able to stop time in its tracks to give us what we needed most—the thing itself. Everything about this situation was dependent on time and I needed it to stop—to stand still. Even my nightmares were haunted by time. I would awaken from a seemingly sleepless night, awash in sweat.

"I've got it, I've got it… this will fix everything" was the mantra of a dream that left me quaking as, in the dream, a doctor would rush into our room with the "cure" seconds after death. It was madness to be sure. But it was my fool's way of trying to control the uncontrollable.

I couldn't control time, but I did discover something about it. At its best, "time" teaches us about love; about the importance of being present in everything we do; it gives meaning to our lives. It separates the real from the imagined and puts all things into perspective. We spend our lives in waiting—as if all meaning can only be assigned or reserved for something yet to be. Even worse, we spend our time as if there will always be more—such a wasteful extravagance. Living in the past seems to occupy half of our days and the other half is filled with dreams for our future. Our present gets lost in the regret of our past and the hope for our future.

Being there, in that place of not enough time, turned all that on its head. I began to view time in a totally different way—time was now reversed. Knowing there wasn't much left gave our lives—what was left of them—such monumental proportion and significance, I would have begged, borrowed, or stolen whatever was required of me to be given more. But time doesn't negotiate. Having to check at the door my pretense of being in control of "time" meant that I would have to accept, that I could not escape from the fact that there would be an endpoint. Living from that impending endpoint backwards to the present left me clinging to the hope that every day would be of consequence and every word, every gesture, every thought, every "look" would be worth far more than I could ever have imagined. Thinking we are invincible, that we have all the time in the world, keeps us from seeing time in reverse. I didn't have that luxury now. Time was closing in on us. And all I could see was the end of everything. Time had done its job and given me insight into what it really was–an unstoppable thing that really did have an endpoint in the physical world. I began to break up every day into moments and every moment into lifetimes of living. But even moments have endings.

Meanwhile, all of us there, surrounded by the constant fear of "we're next," began to separate ourselves from anyone who was not "one of the originals." And every day I, like my neighbors in this place of "not enough time," would anxiously wait for the hushed voices of the physicians and hope the door they entered—and then closed—would not belong to us.

So, while I waited, I played with time. And I would soon find out that it was always one move ahead of me. I took its queen but it would eventually take my king.

Funny the way time plays with you—until it doesn't want to play anymore.

CHAPTER 10:
DEATH REMEMBERED ME

The day started early, as all days of the last seven months had started, with a wakeup call of crash carts and white coats disappearing into rooms up and down the hallway. Not being able to sleep, or not wanting to sleep, had left me physically exhausted and emotionally fragile during those early morning rituals. To wake from a sleepless night seemed a contradiction but everything in this place was turned upside down and inside out and being awake while asleep made perfect sense. Day after day, the fear that the crash carts were coming for us started each morning off with a heightened sense of anxiety. I always felt as though I was falling; it took me a few minutes to regain my footing so I could stabilize my thoughts enough to smile at this man who needed me to smile. Sitting there, with my life wrapped around his, I wondered if it was death itself that I feared, or the fear itself—the waiting for what I knew was inevitable. There was a difference.

Our neighbors in the adjoining rooms had lost their battles one by one and we were one of only two left of the original "gang" of six families. I kept to myself more and more every day—I didn't want to get close to anyone again. I had no strength left to give to anyone outside of this room. Exhausted and anxious, I could do nothing except sit and stare into the depths of what was now our whole world.

I had fallen into the habit of just watching him sleep. I had learned how to count his respirations, which I did a thousand times a day: "one, two, three." My breath hesitated when his did, and then I would sit for what seemed like an eternity waiting for his breathing to normalize before I would breathe again. I knew the patterns of his breathing and had familiarized myself with what each one meant—either pain, or nausea, or fear, or nightmares—and could respond appropriately with meds or words, or water, or whatever was needed to take "it" away. What I could not do, however, was the one thing that he, and I, needed most—touch him. His every nerve ending was on fire and any touch turned his body into a raging inferno. So we would just smile and pretend that neither of us needed that "touch." I had become an expert in pretense but it was becoming so very difficult to hide behind the smile that tried to convince him—and me—that life was anything except cruel.

I was unable to accept our reality—what was happening to him, to me, to our life together. I had no hope of his recovery, but the mere thought of "consenting" to Steve's fate could send me into a rage. To me, acceptance was nothing more than a truly messy emotion that I could never imagine becoming part of my thinking. I could feel my face actually change shape when I thought of "acceptance;" it would morph into a mask of hatred and sarcasm. My eyes would turn cold and my body would tense up into a "flight or fight" mode. So I avoided it; I pushed all thoughts of it so far away from my waking moments, it simply did not exist for me.

Monotony became the name of the game for me—and it was good. We could do monotony and survive. Just going through the motions of everyday living was somehow comforting. No news was good news. "No change" was what I wanted to hear from anyone who opened our door. I had learned to love "boring" – to me, it meant stability. I resisted anything that even smacked of change.

But this day, something was off. His breathing was all wrong and I didn't like it. I didn't know this pattern, and not knowing was unacceptable. Not being able to count these breaths as I'd been doing for months turned my heart to ice—and I froze. His respirations were so uneven, so halting, and just so different from all the times I counted "one, two, three..." I didn't want different. I didn't know how to deal with different. My mind jumped backward to another time when breathing for someone else was all I wanted to do and I tried to remember just how I had accomplished that—until I realized, like a punch in the gut, that I had failed in that effort too.

Adrenaline rushed to my head and I started yelling for a nurse, for anyone to come save us. Just come save us. I would not accept this. Never. There was no time, there would never be enough time and, as the nurse rushed in, I grabbed her by her arm and screamed "Fix this!"

I knew there would be no haven to escape to, no warning to "get ready," no time for acceptance of any type, no room for me to slam the door and knock reality on its ass. I could do nothing but stand there—just stand there—frozen in place and watching as time began to run out.

This was to be his last day. "Acceptance" had taken "no" for an answer for far too long. The door had swung wide open and my fear was making itself known. It was here and now and the crash carts were coming for us.

Standing silently beside the open door, I watched as one physician after another ran in, then turned and walked out. Some looked at me, others didn't. Not wanting to hear what they said but wanting to know and understand every word spoken did nothing but fill my head with noise and confusion. I heard the word "stroke" followed by "tumor breaking up" and "blind, deaf, paralyzed" … words that didn't register in my brain or, if they did, could not possibly have anything to do with us. Had our reality brought us to this place of complete disbelief; had our reality taken from us our right to say goodbye in any real sense? Had I waited too long to accept this nightmare as our own? Standing there watching this, taking it all in, all at once—how was I to do this? Backed up, literally, against a wall now, I tried to speak to our oncologist, and what came out was non-intelligible. So he just reached for me, held me for a while and when he spoke, I listened.

I had heard correctly. The main tumor had broken apart and travelled to his brain, leaving him blind. Those beautiful almond eyes could no longer see, and all I could do was close my eyes and sob. I tried desperately to closet my sobs in my sleeves but the next words I heard were "He can no longer hear you."

The primal scream that escaped from my soul was one I knew so well. Absolutely no sound—only pain, so pure and debilitating that I thought I would stop breathing. Realizing that he could no longer see me or hear me was so intensely shattering. Not just for me—but for him. I imagined the pain he felt in his now silent and darkened world and every part of me ached for him. All I wanted to do was touch him—and, as my arms reached for him, I heard the word "paralyzed' and "he can't feel you." Such a strange comfort came from knowing he couldn't feel my touch. For the first time in months, I climbed into his bed, held him tightly in my arms, kissed him on his beautiful face, stroked his black hair away from his now-closed eyes, and breathed his smell into my lungs so deeply that it became my own.

This was surely Hell. An invention of some god somewhere bent on the destruction of anyone who dares to question the concept of a being who creates only goodness and love. We had fallen into a ravine and this god was throwing rocks at us. Malice was at the heart of this god intent on destruction, and we were his target.

I held so tightly onto what was left of Steve's life. Pouring out all of my strength into his body was my last hope of saving his life. But even as I felt this great love for him, I could feel the rage growing in my soul and I lashed out, once again, in one last-ditch effort to get the attention of whatever God was out there. This God, who seemed to be willing this on us because of my stubbornness and denial of anything that hinted at His existence.

There was a dichotomy in my heart: I wanted to believe in God—to know that there was more to life than just suffering and pain. But I also didn't want to believe – because if He existed, it would mean He was evil for doing this to us—for not healing Steve.

In the end, I did blame God—but how could I blame him if I didn't believe He was real? One thing I absolutely did believe – in the unlikely possibility that He *was* real, I wanted Him to feel my hatred of Him.

Closing my eyes, I tried to sleep. I didn't want to think about anything except this man in my arms. But death was knocking at our door and whispering to me. I had heard these whispers before and knew that I was powerless against them. I felt like laughing at the futility of all life, at the complete and utter vulnerability of life when confronted with this death thing. All the games I had played with myself in the effort to beat the unbeatable seemed like such a waste of time and now, confronted with this new reality, I hated myself for trying to conquer what was inevitable. The time I had wasted on false hope and belief in my own lies seemed to mock me as I finally was forced to look at our situation. I felt stupid and powerless as I realized the time I had spent on nonsensical things could never be retrieved or re-lived. I needed to say things that needed to be heard. I needed to look into his eyes and have him look back at me as I told him everything I should have told him when I had the chance.

But all I could do now was hold him and wait. I could not wish us out of this, or will us out of this, or think us out of this. So, I waited and watched as he clung to life. My sorrow met his silence and the world spun out of control. I was holding tightly to him, trying to ignore the breathing that I didn't recognize and the sounds that filled the room—sounds of his dying. I wanted to be alone with him—but, at the same time, I was afraid of being alone. I didn't want either of us to be here but here we were.

I needn't have feared being alone. Our room had turned into a virtual meeting place for physicians and nurses. They ignored me as I ignored them. It was per-fectly clear to everyone involved that I didn't want any interaction with anyone. Listening to the sometimes hushed remarks about "his condition" left me speech-less at times. I just watched as the progression of white coats listened to his breathing, took his vitals, then turned and walked away. There were vague smiles and looks of concern directed towards me but I would close my eyes and they would leave us alone. I didn't want to listen to their very simple, uncomplicated message – he was dying. And soon.

Death. I knew him intimately. Having introduced himself to me years earlier, he didn't feel the need to make any further introductions. Fear of him grasped my heart and I willed myself to sleep, if only for a short time. I could then quite possibly dream a new dream and find some comfort somewhere in all the lies that still lived in my heart, lies that had sustained us in our daily need for survival. Even now, I wouldn't give in to what was right smack in front of me. But death wasn't having any of it; it invaded my thoughts while pushing out any and every competing thought or emotion.

Gathering every bit of strength left in me, I knew I needed to confront this thing that had grabbed my love from me and was pulling him, breath by breath, down into that pit of Hell where he lived—just waiting for his next victim. I needed to confront him. Somehow, I needed to confront him and explain to him exactly why he needed to leave empty-handed.

There was only one way to accomplish this. I knew I had to talk to God but I didn't know how. It had been decades since I'd spoken even one kind or loving word to Him. I had heaped profanity upon Him and truly meant it. I had denied His existence and truly believed it. I believed Him to be, if He even existed, cold and cruel and unnervingly absent for me. How to start a conversation with someone who I didn't believe existed, or who did exist—but not in any loving, caring way—left me clueless. I had nothing to guide me, nothing to point the way. But, for this man in my arms, I needed to try.

I didn't know exactly who to talk to—God? Death? Were they one and the same? I struggled for answers, but there was one thing I knew for sure: death was real. And if God and death were one and the same, then God did surely exist. I would meet Death again—here and now, in conversation. Would he listen and take my appeal to heart? There was only one way to find out. But where to start?

By then, the activity in our room had picked up and, as the night closed in, I could see the anxiety on the faces of those who glanced at us. Those who had been with us since the beginning tried to hide their feelings and stay "professional," their eyes hardening. Some sat in the corner chair for a while, searching for just the right words; some sat on the cot, using my pillow for support or for a prop, of sorts, to separate themselves from us. Wanting to get close but keeping their distance with a pillow was an act of self-defense that seemed to make some sense in this senseless situation. Some smiled, some spoke to me softly about my "taking care of myself" and some just sat quietly until they felt the tears fall—then exited the room as quickly as they could, thinking I didn't see their tears. I saw them. I saw them all. And I felt it all.

I was grateful when someone would tell me that Steve didn't hear them or feel the sting of their words. But gratitude would die away when I would feel his body tremble under my touch. I knew he was "there," listening and feeling regardless of what the physicians were saying. And death was there...watching and waiting for the moment when he could reach out and take my love from me. This was heartache. This was heartbreak so real it manifested itself as intense physical pain—an actual physical pain that took my breath away, as well as my will to fight any longer.

My denial of this reality had finally caught up with me. The powerlessness, the helplessness, the anger and despair flooded my body and soul so much so that all I could think about was the tragic senseless nature of death. Here, on the edge of Steve's human existence, my emotional and physical struggles shook hands and competed for that blue ribbon. My emotional self said "Give it up, my love. It's okay." My physical self said, "I need you here. I need your touch." Time, or the lack of time, had made life so precious that I didn't know who should win the prize. But here, now, death was coming and all that preciousness was going to slip into oblivion. I could not "believe" my way out of this. I couldn't feel my way out of this. I had to go through this with him. I could not generate a force more powerful than the one waiting for him just on the other side of that one last breath.

Surrender began to flow through me. I had to surrender a love that had surpassed all human understanding to an entity that I had no power to defeat. My heart and mind were broken and I had no choice but to give in to this shadow that my love wore on his face.

We were standing at the precipice of life and death. I had set myself up in competition and conflict with the force that had the control and power all along. This damnation, this waiting game, this pain and suffering—for what? Every time his body would tremble in my arms I would quake from the anger I felt and cry out silently, hoping, wishing, pleading for reprieve. But each time I cried out for reprieve—it didn't come. And my anger would return and I would, once again, curse the very force that could bring the reprieve I longed and wished for.

The line between life and death was blurring. I wondered if great love was actually worth the great despair of loss. I knew that Death had remembered me and it felt as if he was laughing at me. I told myself "let him laugh." I was willing to meet him face to face and dare him to look away. I wanted to be Steve's hero, my own hero, and face down death itself. But every time I felt my love's body tremble, I would lose my resolve and the grief and sadness would take the place of any perceived courage.

All I could do, really, was be still and silent and wait. This day wasn't over yet. His pain wasn't over yet. How many more hours would my love have to endure before Death snatched him away? Our continued dance with death seemed to be never ending. Wishing for a reprieve or for an ending became the same wish. Life and death merged into oneness—and I couldn't tell the difference any longer.

Closing my eyes and wishing for—inviting—oblivion wasn't an option.

But I wished for it anyway.

CHAPTER 11:
BECOMING STARLIGHT

Have you ever looked up at the night sky and wished upon a star? Most of us, at one time or another, have done exactly that. Why? Maybe we were thinking of a Disney song from childhood, or perhaps it came from a longing deep in our soul. Whatever it was, we just naturally looked up and wished for our heart's desire.

I used to do that quite often. When I'd gaze upward, one particular star would always grab my attention—it might have been part of a particular pattern, or perhaps it just twinkled brighter than the others. But one of them always stood out as if to say, "Here I am—now make that wish."

I don't do that anymore. Now when I look upwards on a starlit night, I smile. I remember. And when I wish—it's a wish of a completely different nature. What used to be a childish hope has become a yearning to return home again—to my home within Starlight.

Let me explain. If I had one wish that would come true, it would be that I was a much wiser woman with access to every thought ever had by man and every language ever spoken. I would then be able to string together the words to describe the beauty and majesty of the Shared Death Experience. But I am not that wise, all-knowing woman—so all I can do is give you the very best of what I have at my disposal.

Death comes in many forms. Most times, it comes as predicted and takes your grandparents and parents—in that order and in the manner expected—via old age or illness that comes of aging. But sometimes it comes stealthfully, silently, and catches you unaware—robbing you of your very breath, leaving you gasping for understanding and begging for reprieve. Such was my first meeting with death when he came and snatched the life of my first-born child. Nothing had prepared me for that "meeting" or for the possibility that death could come so unexpectedly. I was left staggering and alone, in despair—a despair that I had not recovered from when I met him again.

The darkness that lay hidden in my Soul revealed itself once again when, as I watched in horror, life slipped from the man who was my husband. Unbridled fear was my constant companion and I knew that, once again, Death was waiting just on the other side of our humanity.

I had lived in fear of something I had no control over and raged at all things good because of my lack of power—or should I say my *powerlessness*. But I knew the day had arrived when I would either step up or fall down in defeat.

I never left his side. The day turned into a series of my reliving every conversation I'd ever had with every single one of his physicians. Every single word spoken played on a continuous loop in my brain in an effort to re-hear or recall anything that I may have originally missed, anything that could pull us off the path we were heading down at lightning speed. Somehow I would drift off into a fitful sleep, still holding him in my arms, and then wake with a jolt because of a dream in which I'd found "the answer." Waking from a dream and realizing it was just a dream would bring tears to my eyes, and I'd fall back into despair. Steve was seemingly oblivious to my machinations as he "slept" in his closed-off and now totally private world.

As the night closed in on us, my mom and dad came in to sit and to "check up" on us. They brought something for me to eat but food was the last thing on my mind. Our oncologist, who by then had become a close friend and confidant, arrived a bit later and took up residence on the cot that still held my body's outline. I didn't speak, nor did anyone else, for there really wasn't anything to be said. Except for the hum of the machines and the normal sounds of life in a hospital, it was quiet—my own personal hell.

I'd been in his bed, with my arms around him, for hours—an entire day, actually. My body was screaming for me to move, if even a little, to relieve the spasms that had been at play in my legs for hours. But I had no intent of letting him go.

I would lie there. I would breathe for him as long as he needed me to. I would not leave his side unless forced to do so because of some element that would present itself to us–an element of reprieve for him. But as the night wore on, our oncologist rose and asked me, very gently, if I would consider letting him hold Steve for a while so he could listen to his heart and check his vitals. I reluctantly agreed and released my hold on him. As I rose, I became aware of the nagging pain in my belly— a pain I realized was born of necessity. So, I ran to the bathroom and, closing the door, flicked on the bathroom light. I glanced into the mirror and wondered just who that gaunt, sunken eyed woman was staring back at me. I didn't recognize myself, and it made me shudder to realize that I'd become someone or something that I didn't know. As I turned to flick off the light, I heard someone cry out. Throwing open the door, I raced back towards the bed, where Steve had rolled over and opened his eyes.

This was the moment I had waited for all day. He'd have his reprieve and I could then tell everyone just how wrong they had been! It was the moment my fear would be replaced with "I told you so's" and rallies of health. I knelt down on the floor at his side so we would be face to face, forehead to forehead. When I saw his glistening eyes looking into mine, tears flooded my own eyes and as I felt them cascade down my cheeks, I smiled. Forehead to forehead, nose to nose, mouth to mouth, and breath to breath, our tears mingled—we were closer to each other in that moment than we'd ever been in our lives. I smiled inwardly, sighed deeply and waited—waited for something, anything, nothing—I wasn't sure exactly what I was waiting for. Then he spoke…

"I just want to remember" came so softly and so sweetly from his lips—it took my breath away. As I gasped at this statement, I breathed in hard and fast—I took in his breath and felt it flow deeply into my lungs, warming me as it travelled into my very spirit. I looked into his eyes expecting and hoping to see my love reflected there, wishing to see a renewing of life. I was so full of expectation and deep longing. But instead, I saw that his beautiful almond eyes had gone dark. I couldn't speak or even move. The scream that escaped from my soul was unheard by any human ear; only a heaven, if one existed, could've heard it. I cried out to a God that I knew wouldn't hear me, a God that I knew didn't exist for me, a God that—if He did exist—could fix all this with a mere thought. This was all so futile, so meaningless, so wrong on every level. It was then I realized I had breathed in my love's last breath, and my knees buckled and I fell to the floor.

I lay there, on that cold tile floor, as a mix of despair and anger, hatred and rage flowed through me. I raged at life, at the ways of the world, at everyone and everything that was alive and well, smiling or laughing or loving. The physical pain that consumed my body came from an overwhelming spiritual and emotional emptiness. What was this all for? Thirty-three years on this earth and he was gone. In less than an instant, he was just gone. I felt as if my very life was now threatened and I lost the ability to speak, to walk, to stand, to even scream out loud at the absolute nothingness that was this universe.

My mind raced. I felt dizzy and flushed. My world had begun to shift somehow and I felt "off" just a notch from the physical world I lived in. It was a space between thought and reality that was real—but wasn't real. I don't know how long I lay there, on the floor on my knees. But at some point, I rose to a standing position, powered by some force of will not my own. Standing there, my world spun out of focus. The floor had disappeared and become mist even as I stood upon it. The wall and window turned to mist, as well. Suddenly, the room's confines were surreal—not there, but still there. I watched as the ceiling floated above me—and it was in that moment that I noticed the stars.

So many stars—it was as if a billion stars had come to collect me. I could see each and every one of them, separate and distinct in and of themselves, but, at the same time, all part of one whole—one enormous— pure light. The light itself wasn't white or really any color I could ever describe—just purity as I imagine purity would be on the first day of the universe. I shouldn't have been able to look at this light without being blinded—but it was so comforting and so inviting that I felt myself being drawn inside. I went freely. These stars had an inviting presence, and I wanted to lose myself within them. I felt a sense of belonging to something that I didn't quite understand—but did understand on some deeper level—a level untouched and unknown for all of my thirty years on this earth. Time slowed to nothingness; I found that it was no longer a function of my reality. I had no idea what was happening to me or what I was witnessing—I only knew that it was "right."

I felt like dancing within the light, and I found myself being twirled round and round so quickly that I couldn't see where I was, as if I'd been blindfolded. Was this a game of hide and seek within the light?

Then the spinning stopped, and I saw him—alive and well. Within that Starlight stood my love. I tried to focus my eyes on him and on nothing else. There he was, smiling at me, not speaking—so I spoke. "I can see you!" I said. Again, he just smiled at me—a smile so full of joy I thought I would cry. But I found that there were no tears in me—only joy. He stood before me, and I before him, each wanting to hold and comfort the other. But, despite this yearning, we each knew, somehow, that we were exactly where we were supposed to be. He was at peace, but it was more than just peace. I have no words for what it was—he just "WAS."

The look on his face as he watched me was so full of love. But I could see that he recognized all that was happening to him—and to me.

In this place, I was being supported by some unseen presence, held by something or someone that was incredibly loving and filled with compassion for me. I knew I was breathing but it felt as if someone was breathing for me. The stars were still there, warming me and cocooning me, holding me up with such tenderness that somehow being there felt more natural than anything I'd ever experienced. I relaxed into the light and it became one with me—or did I become one with it? I simply do not know. All I knew was that where I ended, the light began, and where the light ended—I began. I was there, alive within starlight.

I had become Starlight.

I was more aware of myself than I had ever been in my entire life. I knew everything was exactly the way it was supposed to be. Standing there, being held there, in that place of perfect peace, I felt a recognition of all that I was, all that he was, all that simply "was."

And there was something else: a knowledge that I'd been there before—cradled in that place of love. The feeling was an old one, a long-ago, forgotten memory that had lain untouched and unrealized in my soul since the day I was born. In this place, held by a magnificence that was somehow mine—I finally rested.

I knew I was in the presence of the One who formed me with His hands and His thoughts before the very beginning of time. I was in the presence of my God. He was the presence within the stars. It was His light that held me up. It was He who'd sent the stars to collect me, to gather me to Him. It was His love and His compassion that had blessed me with this journey—where I could see and know that my beloveds were safe and secure, alive and well at home with Him—where we all began.

I felt safe in this place that seemed to be offering me forgiveness and unconditional love, but I was also confused and dazed. How long I would be allowed to stay—I didn't know. Staying became uppermost in my mind and I forgot all else for a while.

I did sense, somehow, that Steve would not be staying with me. He would be going away, moving to a place where I would not be allowed to follow. And in due time, or something like time, I saw him drifting away. His smile changed and he wore upon his face an expression so gentle, so loving—I knew it had to mean "goodbye." As his face faded from my view, I didn't feel pain or grief—rather, I felt my Soul fill up with gratitude and love for a man who had given me the greatest gift, one I could never have imagined—a peek into forever-ness and always. It seemed inexplicable, but I just "stood" there—not reaching for him or expecting anything from him. The serenity and purity of that place filled my soul and I simply closed my eyes.

I didn't question what was happening or even why it was happening. I knew I was meant to be a part of all this. I also knew that Steve was alive and well in this place of forever and, with that knowledge, I let go of the fear and grief and rage that had been my constant companion for so many years. Or, more specifically, it was taken from me.

Emptied of all my grief and rage, I had become one with the light, one with my God, and one with the purpose He had laid out for me before all time. I felt more whole, more forgiven than I'd ever felt before. I now felt nothing except an all-encompassing love and compassion. My heart held no fear, no anger, no grief, no struggle. I was complete just as I was—I lacked nothing. Deep down, I suppose I had always known this; I had just forgotten it for a while.

How long I was held there after Steve disappeared from my view—I don't know. I just rested in the strength and all-consuming love that held me so closely. But eventually, the light started to fade and I felt myself shifting back to whatever reality was waiting for me. Leaving that place was not my decision—I was given no choice but to return to my existence—and I soon found myself standing firmly upon a solid floor in a hospital room lit with dingy fluorescent lights. The stars still shone in a picture window that encompassed one full wall, and my eyes and heart searched desperately for that one pinpoint of light that would still speak to me—but I couldn't find it again.

I was determined to stay focused and remember all that had happened. I closed my eyes and memorized the feeling—as if that were even a possibility. As the stars left me, deposited me back into the physical world that I knew, I felt saddened and more alone than I'd ever felt in my life. Leaving that place of Grace, that place where time stood still—or did not exist at all—made me feel as if I was dying.

To say that I'd surpassed all human emotion doesn't make much sense, I know. But my experience is so very difficult to explain because no words exist to paint the picture as beautifully and as pure as it should be painted. How do I describe going beyond pain and rage, passing through joy and serenity on the way to a peace that can never be described? How does one describe a feeling beyond joy, beyond ecstasy, beyond any imagining of our humanity? I don't have the words at my disposal, either then or now, and even if I could, the very act of defining and categorizing the feeling would, essentially, diminish the entirety of the experience. Being alive within Starlight—together with eternity—is there a word for that? I think not.

In being held and caressed in that place and losing the "me" that I'd believed myself to be, allowed me to become the "me" that existed before time and space formed my very being. My peek into the forever-ness of all things—into myself—was as confusing as it was full of Grace. Trying to understand all that happened was tantamount to wrestling a crocodile without having any arms. The only thing I understood was that Steve was alive and well and at peace, and that my experience had saved my life.

When I try to imagine what lay beyond Starlight, the place where Steve was going when he left my sight, the place where our Stephanie was waiting for him— my heart and Soul just soared. I knew that I couldn't go there, wouldn't be allowed to follow no matter how much I wished to be there. I had no power or purpose there—this experience was given to me as a gift. I knew I didn't belong there, nor could I overstay my welcome. When it was time for me to go, it was time, and there was nothing I could do or say to prolong my stay or head off my departure.

But soon, it would be time for another type of departure. It would soon be time for me to leave my life in the hospital behind and return home to a life with my little boy. I prayed that he would be sound asleep and wouldn't awaken when I arrived home. That night, I didn't feel equipped to face him and tell him that his daddy would never be coming home. So I fervently prayed to a God that I now knew was with me always and asked for a reprieve till morning. My boy was far too young to understand the events that had taken place this night, so I knew I had to find just the right words—if that was even possible. I closed my eyes as I left this world of sadness and grief behind me and, once again, prayed for the strength I would need to face the morning.

The ride home was warm and silent. Sitting in the back seat of my parents' car, thinking about my little boy, thinking about his daddy, I looked up at the stars and asked for help. I looked at them through a different lens now, through knowing eyes, and I cried. I cried because I now belonged to them, and they belonged to me. I cried as I thanked Steve for loving me so much. I cried and thanked God for taking me to Him and I thanked Him for all that He was and for all he He'd given me on this night. I cried as I felt myself giving way to the grief that came not only from losing Steve but from returning to a life where I would lose that indescribable feeling of Grace, where my humanity would smack me in the face time and time again just from living my life. But at that moment, when I was feeling exceptionally sorry for myself, the breeze of a beautiful star-filled April night caressed my face from the open window—and I stopped crying. I just stared up at the stars and felt something I'd never felt before when looking at the night sky: homesick.

As I smelled the deliciousness of the fresh air outside the car window, I locked my eyes upon the brightest star I could find—and wished one final seemingly childish wish; I wished for home. Then the thought came to me—which home, I wondered? Could I possibly live in them both?

I remember smiling at the possibility.

Chapter 12:
Let Me Tell You a Story

My self-imposed descent into darkness began after the loss of my child. It was then that I chose to create and live in a world where my emotions never stopped trying to beat me up. I told myself to push away any thoughts that would keep me separated from joy and peace, but no matter how hard I tried, my heart remained full of nightmarish images. I felt death every second of every minute of every day. The emotions and pains that coursed through my body made it difficult to even breathe, and at times, it felt as if my heart would just stop beating.

Contrary to popular cliché, we don't ever just "get over" the tragedies of life. Rising above these tragedies is such an alien concept—but "rise above" is exactly what I heard from so many well-meaning friends. At every opportunity, they would say, "Just rise above it"—as if that were even possible. "Just rise above it" always seemed to be followed by "Time heals all wounds." I would just smile and turn away. And never be around them again. Navigating that world became like moving through a maze of near misses in a minefield—every time I would start to feel anything other than grief, I would be pulled backwards into that same pit of isolation and pain. Time wasn't healing anything and there was no place to "rise to."

In my anguish, I'd blocked out everything that didn't speak to my pain. I paid no attention to the everyday gifts that presented themselves to me; people that really mattered; words that could've lifted me up and taken me back to a happier time; and fleeting memories that would've reminded me of something my dad had given me long ago. My dad was a storyteller, a weaver of tall tales and fantasy. Within those tales, he wove the truth of the universe as he saw it and knew it. His tales were all metaphors for life and spoke to the intrinsic nature of all things. It seems unfathomable to me, as I look back, that I could have forgotten one story in particular—a tale that was a metaphor for the very nature of God Himself. But forget it I did, like smoke hitting the blades of a fan. Recovering that lost treasure, that gift given to me and to my sisters, took me back to a time when, sitting on my dad's lap—he taught me about love.

So, come now, back to that moment when all things were right and good. Suspend your adulthood for a while and travel back to the easier times and the days of innocence.

Let me tell you a story…

Once upon a time, there was a little girl who just ached to always be outdoors. One morning, as she woke to see a beautiful day, she stretched out her arms and jumped gleefully out of her bed to greet the morning sunshine. She quickly washed her face, brushed her hair and half-heartedly brushed her teeth—what was left of them anyway!

Running downstairs, she listened for the sound of her dad milling around somewhere in the home they shared with her sisters. Her dad heard her and turned to greet her with a smile that spoke volumes, and she ran to him to get her first hug of the day. After a quick breakfast, she asked him if she could go outside to play. Of course, he said "yes" and after the usual "be care-ful's," she threw open the door and ran outside with carefree abandon. As she dashed off to explore her world, she turned and waved goodbye to her dad, who stood at the doorway. She heard him yell, "I love you, honey. Have fun!"

What an amazingly beautiful day it was for explora-tion. And explore was exactly the thing that was on her mind that day. She went immediately to the new play-ground and slid down slides of all heights and designs, climbed on the monkey bars and played in the sand box till her shoes and clothes were full of sand.

Brushing herself off and tiring of the playground, she started to think about newer and bigger adventures that lay just on the other side of the pasture, where her grandmother lived. Losing sight of her home once she crossed the pasture was nothing new to her and caused her little if no fear at all. She knew her way home. And today, she was remembering the newly grown watermelons in her grandma's garden; being quite hungry, she ran to the farm and ate her fill. Watermelon juice oozed down her clothes and skin, making her all sticky. Her face tasted sweet long after she'd finished eating.

She made a beeline for the stream that meandered throughout the farm and fields and waded in – waist deep—cleaning her face, hands, and clothes until she felt "not sticky." Climbing out of the stream with nothing to dry herself off, she drip-dried, leaving mud puddles. The puddles were just too inviting to avoid, so in she went for a good stomping. All day long she played in the stream and the fields with animals of every description and with any child that she would encounter.

She knew some of the other children, but some she had never seen before; she was so excited to be making new friends. Some were just like her, others completely different—and from far off lands she could only imagine.

For hours they lived in a fairy tale of her own making where everyone was a member of her royal court. She would knight them all with her mighty sword, hewn from the fallen branch of a Sycamore tree that adorned the river bank. Princes and kings were at her command. A crown of field flowers, growing wild and free, flowed from her hair and she imagined herself beautiful.

But as the light began to fade into darkness, she decided to begin her journey back home. Leaving her kingdom behind, she told every living creature that she would return in the morn. The morning glories closed their eyes and the animals, one by one, lay their heads down to sleep.

She was still very far from home, so she quickened her step, knowing that her dad would be watching and waiting for her return. Her eyes scanned the darkening sky, looking for the beams of the porch light her dad always turned on for her return, lest she lose her way in the darkness. Listening for his voice, she heard his calls: "Honey, it's time to come home! Come quickly for the night is falling and I need you safely at home. Come home now, honey. I'm waiting at the door."

Hearing his voice and seeing the light, the little girl ran as fast as her short, tiny legs would carry her. As she spied her house, she quickened her pace even more, excited to jump into the waiting arms of her dad. So excited to tell him of her day, she forgot all about the state of her dress or the mud that had dried and caked over her entire being. She was scratched and bruised from her falls and jousting tournaments and her hair still held the wild flowers she had plucked from the ground. But she ran to her dad—unafraid and smiling. He had been waiting patiently at the door with out-stretched arms strong enough to catch her as she leaped into them.

He wrapped his arms around her, kissed her dirty face, and carried her into the house and over to the massive armchair where he always sat. He sat her upon his lap, not caring one bit about the muddy, dirty, pile that was his daughter, and held her tiny hands in his. Just one question was on his mind. As the love he felt for his child brought a smile to his face, he spoke: "So, tell me about your day, my darling."

As he listened intently and held her close, he smiled once again. A smile so full of love, the little girl cried and held him as tightly as she could. Putting a finger under her chin, he said so softly and with such love, "My darling, you've had such a long adventurous day, but now the night has fallen and it's time for you to rest." When she started to complain about what she would miss when asleep and how, sometimes, she would wake in the darkness feeling lonely and afraid, he said, "The morning will be here soon enough. Let today take care of today, and let the night hold no terrors for you. Never fear, my darling, I will be right next to you all through the night and I will be the first person you see when you open your eyes in the light of the new morning." She closed her eyes and, as he held her close to his heart— she slept.

The pure simplicity of the truth concealed in my dad's story is like the line from scripture: "Suffer the little children to come unto me," a line that now makes perfect sense to me. My dad was not a religious man, nor was he someone to shy away from what he perceived to be truth. He was a military man and learned much about life from the three wars he fought in. Those wars had such a huge impact on him, and he struggled for years trying to "fit it all together" in a way that made sense. The senseless loss of life, the fighting and dying and unabated grief of war left him with a gaping hole in his spirit. He needed to fill that hole with the truth, as he would discover it for himself through years of searching for his answers.

Growing up with this man as my father was one of the greatest joys of my life. The love he gave to me through his stories, with his time and attention, with his always-abiding presence made my childhood a safe place for my imagination to flourish and for me to realize my dreams without judgment or condemnation.

But as usually happens when someone "grows up," I left behind the stories, the imagination, and many of the dreams I had in my childhood. If I'd remembered that story–that profound tale—I could've found what I needed, that same childhood innocence that took me into the very arms of an always present, loving God.

Losing that childhood innocence happens to all of us, unfortunately. Call it ego, false intellect, selfishness, or just plain "growing up," but we let go of those things that no longer seem to serve our wants and needs. The world grabs us by the throat and forces us to perceive life in a "grown up" way, and holding onto childhood dreams and treasures just doesn't fit into the whole scheme of adulthood. Why is it that we feel the need to let go of those things that filled our childhood hearts with joy and replace them with things that don't fill us with the same joy? Life gets in the way, and we lose ourselves to doubt and fear and all those things that go bump in the night. We lose sight of ourselves—always running away from our true selves, chasing dreams attached to some label we wear on our foreheads, or intellect that will replace childhood foolishness, or the perfect romance, or impossible wealth, or some other "thing" that keeps us distracted from seeing ourselves truly and honestly. We fill our lives with so much "stuff" and add such enormous importance to meaningless objects—that big comfy chair of your childhood gets lost in the hot fast shuffle.

When we then have a tragedy befall us, we have no reserves to fight it. We have lost the innocence that allows us to just "believe" and keep our heads above the waterline. To let go of our childhood—must that entail letting go of our true essence? Perhaps ... but how to find your way back again after the compromises of life have ripped your innocence from you? That's the big question. Letting go of your fear, your unforgiveness, your condemnation of yourself and your judgments about your life is the way to finding yourself and ending the separation that you chose for yourself. Finding that light on the porch, silencing the false intellect that tells you you are on your own allows you to meet "How was your day, my darling?" with childhood innocence once again.

Finding that story again, remembering how it made me feel, was just the beginning of my remembering the other tall tales and fantasies learned at my father's knee. I carry them with me now. They thrive and live in my heart just as the memory of him—the man who lived for me since the day I was born—thrives and lives in my heart. His stories were always meant to teach us about life—the good, the bad and the ugly—but the tale about the girl going out to play was the one he always pointed to as the single most important of all.

It taught me that I was tethered to him just as I was tethered to God. Like the little girl in his story, I always ran home to be with my dad. He would stand watch over me while I slept and keep me safe from harm. As a child, I knew this about my father and never questioned it. But when I grew I started to question everything and put childhood things away to make room for what I thought would "complete" me as an adult. Little did I know that I would need the kind of unquestioning belief I had as a child to survive as an adult.

When God's "Come quickly for the night has fallen"… came into my life as I was losing my loved ones, I should have met the "words" with unwavering acceptance for the love inherent in them—as I did when my dad said them. But now, when it really mattered, when night had really fallen—I met His call with anger and denial, arrogance and a choice of complete separation from all that was good and joyful. I should have known that, just like in my relationship with my dad, there was never anything I could have ever done or said— no betrayal, no compromise, no words or actions that would have ever separated me from God.

Disease and death are both part of life, but in my pain, I simply could not accept that fact. I didn't understand anything about life and death. No one sits us down and has that conversation! We shy away from any discussion that addresses the issues that make us uncomfortable or sad. We simply do not like to think about the fact that those dearest to us die when we least expect it. Growing up believing that life was supposed to be fair and always joyful was naïve and childish. Feeling that I was a victim of God's judgment, that He purposely targeted us, was my way of dealing with something I had never dealt with before—monumental grief. In that grief, I turned from the loving "God" my dad had told me about, and chose to deny His very existence. That, too, was entirely childish, as I now know that, although frayed for a while, the cord that ties me to God will always be unbroken. I should have remembered that when God called.

"Come home now, darling. I'm waiting at the door"... I can still hear my dad's voice and see his smile every time I think of his stories. And this story, just as he said, was truly the most important of all. The porch light, turned on, would glow in the night sky and lead that little girl home to her dad who was always watching and waiting for her.

I understand that now. I understand it all. I found that porch light again, as an adult—I found it in Starlight.

"So, tell me, my darling, how was your day?"

Where do I begin?

Chapter 13:
That Place

Heaven. There are many different words for it in many different languages. And each day, it's a "place" that's referred to more than any other in the world. Why? Every single race, religion, ethnicity, and culture—members of each one believe in the concept of Heaven. Religious scholars and philosophers have debated, argued, and fought over the very nature of Heaven since time immemorial and they have written reams and reams of papers about it and stockpiled book after book on library shelves for millennia.

But it's not the conversations or writings of the religious scholars or philosophers that touch the true nature of "that place." It's the conversations that take place in the hospices, hospitals, ICU's and funerals of the world that take us into the soul of humanity and, therefore – into Heaven. It's in times of great personal trauma that many of these discussions take place. And, sometimes, these private moments can become very heated due to the stress and fear that exist in the trying moments before the death of a loved one. Once the word "Heaven" is spoken out loud, the underlying, unacknowledged, unspoken word that goes with it is death. Fear that death is near—especially in the waiting rooms of the ICU—prompts exchanges that are not normally heard in everyday family life.

When "the end" is near, people shy away from using the word "death"; their conversation will, instead, turn to the "place" where their loved one "is going" and to each person's individual interpretation of exactly what and where Heaven is—and everyone has their own "truth." Listening to, and being part of these conversations, is both joyous and heart wrenching as families try to come to terms with exactly "where" their loved one will be after they die. This conversation is repeated countless times, every single day, all over the globe.

The conflict begins the very minute someone questions the interpretation of another. In these moments of great tragedy, having one's viewpoint understood and accepted as truth—the only truth—is vitally important to each person's peace of mind. Therein lies the problem. The discussion turns to debate—then to all-out disagreement.

I understand the conflict. Over the years, I have shared my SDE with many friends, colleagues, and mentors, and my explanations and descriptions have sometimes caused heated debate among them. I have spoken to individuals from all walks of life, from all the great religions of the world, from every background and school of thought, and every one of them had their own version of what "truth" should "be" or "is." While all their "truths" were different, they did have a unifying thread—a belief in an afterlife. "Heaven" and "Hell" were central to every debate and the descriptions of these "places" were similar in both nature and belief.

In the course of these debates and conversations, I have been asked to explain "where" I was taken, what I meant by "I became Starlight," and to describe exactly what "God" looked like. It is so very difficult to accurately relay my experience because I must rely on "words." To use words such as "majestic, magnificent, purity defined, peaceful, still, home" dulls the experience because of the mere fact that labeling it—using words to describe the indescribable—just doesn't do the SDE justice. To characterize the face of God, the touch of God, is tantamount to explaining perfection itself—how can it be done? How do you depict an emanation of love and joy combined with otherworldly purity? How do you describe an ethereal form that consists of pure light? The "how" lies in the experience itself as given to you by God Himself—His face, His thoughts, His Word engraved upon your heart—how do you give voice to that feeling?

The "how" lies hidden in the vision, the "feeling" of pure Spirit–the soul must feel its way through to see perfection without being polluted by the scripts we grew up identifying with and falling victim to. "God looked like love I have never experienced before" has always been my answer. There are some feelings and thoughts that can never be expressed—words don't exist to describe them. Our own humanity puts locks on the words felt in the Soul. The physicality of God's appearance—it simply wasn't important. I felt absolutely no curiosity about it—His touch was just too all-consuming and comforting to think of anything else. Perhaps one day, someone will invent a word that accurately depicts "the pure light that is love" that will get us one step closer to seeing His perfection.

Once the head shaking stops from my lack of a physical description, the conversation turns to "where" was I? Most organized religion tells us that God is "separate" from us, that He lives somewhere "out there," above the clouds in a place called Heaven. Religion teaches us that God is the creator and final arbiter of the rights and wrongs of living and that we all will surely answer to Him for all our wrong doings. And just as we've been told who and what God is, we've also been told what "heaven" is, in descriptive terms that everyone can visualize. Heaven is a specific place, the likes of which there is no equal. It is an "other" world, out there somewhere, filled with everything wonderful and beautiful, full of creature comforts that we only dream about. Mansions line golden streets encrusted with pearls and diamonds, and everyone has everything they ever wanted—and everyone who was the best "good little boy or girl" has even bigger and better things than those who weren't quite as good in this life. We earn that mansion on that particular street in that particular neighborhood by the things we do or believe or by the things we don't do or don't believe while living on this earth. Sounds like a bigger and better version of life here, doesn't it? I fully accepted that version, that description of Heaven given to me as a child. The innocence of childhood demands "pictures" we can understand. Adjectives that paint a picture of a human paradise comfort and console us when we think of death—ours or anyone else's.

But that is not what I found in "that place" among my stars. Was there physicality, a form, a space—a specific place that could be described? I can't say there was! What I found, and felt, instead, in the place where I was held, was magnificence itself: Pure Starlight—and God Himself. And the most amazing surprise of all—I found the "me" as God intended me to be from the moment He formed me in my mother's womb—before this world got ahold of me and slapped labels on me that told me who to "be" and what to believe. But in "that place," I found myself as a magnificent extension of God. My answer to the question, "What does God look like?" has always been the same: to describe God, I would be describing my own Soul. And to describe "that place" requires a complete letting go of everything that any logic and human reasoning would dictate.

The very essence of God, of Heaven, was in and of that Starlight. I discovered—no, I just knew—that there is nowhere that God is not. He is in and of everything that has ever existed. There is nothing that He is not. There is no place that He is not. If it exists, it is a part of Him— His thoughts created everything, including every one of us. We exist purely because he thought of each one of us. We are the physical forms of His thoughts. We are his creations—part of a whole that we can't perceive. We are all intricately combined as one thought of God but gloriously separate as individuals for some reason unknown to us—but known to Him from the moment He gave each of us life.

To think of one's self as being a part of God, at first blush, seems arrogant and blasphemous. But upon further reflection—it is as natural a thought as breathing. Realizing that it's His breath we breathe takes us further into the truth of all existence—we are all part of the One Who formed us from pure thought and we all represent one aspect of His very Being. I have heard it described as a cup of water drawn from the ocean—one small part of the whole, unchanged from the whole, separate but identical in nature to the whole. The entire ocean is in that cup! Just as the entirety of God Himself lives in our individual Souls. . . . there has never been, nor can there ever be, a separation from God—or from each other—for we are His very thoughts.

As to the questions, "Was I in 'heaven?' " and "Was it God who was holding me so tenderly?", my answer, again, has always been the same. According to every description I had ever heard of or learned about—no and no. There wasn't any shape or form that created any type of boundary that would have said, "This is a place called Heaven." And God—well, having been taught since childhood that God's judgment was fast and sure and His vengeance for wrongdoing was swift—this couldn't possibly be the same "person." But I innately knew this was exactly what I felt it to be! This place where my God was holding me, embracing my soul, had absolutely nothing in common with any "Heaven" I had ever been taught about. If you wish to call it Heaven, then by all means, feel free to do so. I don't. Why? Because by the very nature of giving that place a name, you give it a location—a form and space—which I cannot, and do not, any longer ascribe to. It wasn't—or didn't appear to be—any place in particular, but was, instead, everywhere all at once within Starlight.

Heaven, to me, then, is being in the very presence of God—wherever that happens to be! I found God in the Starlight—was that starlight heaven? I was held by Him in "that place"—was that Heaven? And when Steve disappeared from my view—was he on his way to a different Heaven?

I have only one answer for those questions. Where was I? "That place" was, and is, with and within my God! Period. There were no mansions, no rooms, and no need for anything of any human or physical value. I had no physical form to speak of—but having said that—I was, somehow, essentially a better version of "me." I felt and saw and knew—I knew just who I was and what I was and where I was. As difficult as it is to explain, it is equally as difficult to understand: I was "in" and "of" God. I was one with Him. And that was enough. I was wherever He was—everywhere and nowhere, all at once—in pure light and love.

The problem I have with calling "that place" Heaven, then, is, due to the very word itself—the images it conjures up in our minds puts limits and boundaries on what I found. We imagine a place "out there" somewhere that has a specific physical form. I am, by no means, a religious scholar or a wise philosopher who has made studying Scripture a life-long endeavor. There is, however, one particular verse in Scripture that both comforts and vexes my Soul.

John 14:2 in The Gospel of John in the Holy Scriptures says, "In my Father's house are many mansions ... I go to prepare a place for you." This resonates and rumbles around in my brain, so much so that I am constantly looking for new interpretations that could allow my "Aha" moment to finally settle this question once and for all. Some scholars say Jesus Christ was speaking of Heaven; some say it was allegory or metaphor; some say He was speaking to the fact of "being" with "Him" in some manner not fully explained. I grab hold of the "a place for you," and that has become my definition of Heaven— being with Him, abiding in Him. There is no separation of God and "that place" for they are one and the same. He is "that place" and "that place" is within Him.

I believe I was in "that place" that was meant for me. And "that place" was, and is, with and within my Creator, my God—wherever that happens to be! I do not care if it is a physical "place" or a different dimension, or purely Spirit, or even no place at all! As long as I am in His Presence—that's all that matters! With Him—I do not lose myself. I am a better version of myself having returned home to abide within Him. The dichotomy here is not confusing to me at all—I am part of Him as He designed me to be.

There can be no description of anything else that can or could ever compare to the wonder of just "being" within and cocooned by God. "Heaven," then, becomes a place where form doesn't matter, where location has no meaning, where time and space have no significance at all because Heaven and God are synonymous. I fully understand that humanity requires specifics for comfort; we want "words" to form a vision of the place; to see in our mind's eye where our lost loved ones are. We require something solid to hang our hats on so that "They are now in Heaven" conforms to the norms of our respective cultural definition of Heaven. That seems logical; conformity to cultural definition makes life—and death—easier.

But the reality is quite different. Have you ever had a conversation with someone whose ideas, thoughts, and beliefs are fundamentally different than yours and then thought, "They are so wrong"? Believe me, they are thinking the same thing about your thoughts and beliefs. And just how do each of us resolve the differences without questioning our own? Therein lies one of the oldest foes of humankind. Unfortunately, thinking vs. believing vs. knowing can only be sorted out with the intercession of the one and only Divine Presence of this entire universe—and that takes an awareness and willingness to accept the fact that what we consider "truth" may not be wholly accurate. Ego gets in the way of Spirit and we get lost in translation.

What I thought about truth and what I believed by virtue of my upbringing were most definitely not the same thing as experiencing what I now know will be my truth for the rest of my life.

I thought I knew what Heaven was and where it was. I believed what I thought. I thought I knew who God was and what He was all about. I believed what I thought. Heaven was a place where God cast judgment on sinners. The irony of it was, if anyone deserved to be judged—it would've been me! I denied His very existence. I cursed His name and belittled every single person who expressed belief in a loving God—but there was no judgement for me, only compassion and overwhelming care and concern. Was God judgmental? Nothing could have been farther from the truth as I experienced it on that Starlit night.

"That place" within starlight—that was "heaven"— and because God lives in everything and is everywhere at all times, *He* was that Starlight. There can be no starlight, no heaven, and no "place" without being within and of God Himself.

I understand it's difficult to think of Heaven as not being a literal, physical place, but that's what I found. Even though I knew I was "somewhere" and that somewhere seemed to be "a place" where the overriding feeling was one of Spirit, of Divine Presence, of compassion and love—and "knowing" that I was one with the Presence I felt when the stars came to collect me—I can't say I saw a physical manifestation of Heaven. I was in and of pure light. Call it light, energy, Spirit—whatever you wish—but I was part of something so immense, so magnificent, an adjective to describe it simply does not exist.

Granted, I was held in one place and not allowed to continue further, as Steve did. Was I not allowed to see what lay on the other side of "that place" for a reason? Was "that place" a waiting room of sorts? Quite possibly. But, my mind cannot conceive of a place more comforting or Divine than exactly where I was! And what I was allowed to see was so perfect in Spirit—it changed my life forever. This "knowing," this awareness firmly cemented my spiritual beliefs and has only served to further my deeper search within my own "religious" tradition. There is no contradiction for me between what I now consider truth and the teachings of the One that I know lives within me. So, for the time being, "that place" – be it Heaven or not—exists solely in the absolute Presence of the One True God. I cannot separate the place from the Spirit. Maybe next time around, I will be allowed to have more—if that is even a possibility.

So, when I hear the word "Heaven," I think Spirit.

I believe in what I was shown.

I was shown that Heaven is the "place" where God makes His Presence known. Literal or not—it simply does not matter...

And I know, from experiencing an awareness of Divine Spirit and Presence, that God sometimes grants you just a peek into His Being—to utterly dispel the boogiemen that sometimes inhabit dreams...

CHAPTER 14:
THE UNDOING OF DARKNESS

*"Eye has not seen, nor ear heard, neither has it entered
into the heart of man, that which God has prepared."*
                                        1 Corinthians 2:9

*W*hat exactly is the truth about God and just where do
we fit into that "truth?" Philosophically speaking, what
is *truth? Is there a Divine Wisdom that can be experienced by
mankind and, if yes, is it so incomprehensible that we can't
understand it, even at a basic level?* These were the questions that filled my mind after my SDE.

Clinical and anecdotal research tells us that the Near
Death Experience and the Shared Death Experience
have far-reaching effects on those who are Blessed
enough to have been given these experiences. None
of us who have been given this gift asked for it or did
anything to warrant it—the "why's and how's" remain a
mystery still.

But going to "that place" and sensing the enormity
of all that was given to me left me with a gaping hole in

my Soul—one I needed to fill in order to function in my world. The journey from darkness to light, the "putting it all together" with an understanding that was granted through Grace, occurs within the very heart of hearts. This place is hidden, secreted away from the sufferings and imperfections of humanity—it's where the mystics have long believed that God dwells within us, accessible only to Him and to our awakened selves. Divine wisdom and truth live there; once unlocked, they become the very light that illumes our soul and saves our lives. In finding God and knowing His perfection for the first time, in find-ing our Soul hiding within God, we become that perfect expression, that "perfect thought of God" that brought us into being. We become who He formed us to be, created us to be—a magnificent extension of God Himself.

Before my SDE, I lived in a contemplative night that had lasted for years; allowing no light to shine on my Spirit, I sank deeper and deeper into despair—a despair that I came to identify with and accept as a normal and natural way of being. The groaning of my heart filled my ears, drowning out everything else. I had forgotten all else. I had to get to the point of complete surrender—a total and utter emptying of myself—to make room for a renewal of my Soul, and a true union with a God that I had never known.

Surrender required something that I had never even considered: being still. Stillness had evaded me in recent years; my entire being had been consumed by constant thought, pain, and rage. I never once stopped long enough to take a full and cleansing breath. Whether

I was terrified to breathe deeply and fully or just too engrossed in trying to control life with all its cruelties, I don't know.

There were so many instances where I would have been better served by letting go and listening to the voice inside of me. But I resisted, and no one could have told me that the inner voice I heard wasn't just *me* or my "conscience." I truly had no desire to listen. And I paid a very steep Spiritual price.

The issue at hand was that I misunderstood "surrender." I sensed it would mean failure and defeat. But when I finally did surrender, I found it to be the exact opposite. With surrender came such a stillness—a quieting of my heart and soul that I didn't know was possible. The unimaginable grief of the abyss that swallowed me up seemed to be taking my very life and I felt myself going willingly. I had no fight left in me. It was then that, most likely, I opened myself up to whatever God – the one that I had raged against—had in store for me. I found that within stillness—within surrender (which was diametrically opposed to failure)—came a quieting of body and mind so stark and complete that I wasn't even aware of who I was anymore. It was only then that I would (or could) experience "the peace that surpassed all understanding" and find my way again. It was there that my Starlit night began to make sense. It took no less than a fall from Grace to uncloak the sweetness that was just waiting to engulf me and claim me in love.

The truth of that night took me years to fully understand—if understanding is even possible. Think back to your childhood for just a minute and to your "religious training." I was raised in the church from a very early age. I knew all the prayers, the songs and the "correct" way to think about and approach the God who lived out there in some faraway place called "Heaven." This God needed constant worship and appeasement and any kind of infraction held severe consequences. I was, quite literally, afraid of that God. I had lived a lifetime of reproach, trying with child-like innocence to establish a relationship with a God that I both feared and loved as only a child can. I went to Him wide-eyed and in love because that was expected of me. Anything less would bring down His judgment and, from what I was being taught, His judgment was swift and sure.

In my youth, I believed that God is separate from us, that we are essentially alone, that we must go somewhere to find Him. Whether that thought was forced on me as a child or whether it was created by me, in my own mind, I don't know, but it tended to re-enforce the separateness and aloneness I felt during the tragedies of my life. If God was separate, He could sweep in and shield me from any difficulty in life, right? So why hadn't He done so?

Increasingly, my soul questioned His very existence. Discovering that I had spent a great deal of my life believing in "something" that was imperfect – that wouldn't save me—left me empty and wanting. I had created that "other" from my own thoughts and then I blamed that "other" when it seemed I was deserted. I had convinced myself of such falsities and then blamed that falsity for abandoning me! I left what I believed to be the teachings of the Church.

Looking back, I realized I'd believed that there was a condition to God's protection: I needed to be perfect. I knew that I was indeed, *not* perfect, so I struggled with what I'd been taught from an early age. I came to believe that the only thing that surely did exist was imperfection. It's not surprising that I felt that imperfection was the norm—our natural inclinations take us away from the perfect—away from the one truth of our existence, the truth of who we are. Believing we are separate from God and from each other causes the perfect to crack— and we think that we are, indeed, alone. Nothing could be further from the truth.

My awakening came not from feeling *something*, but, actually, from feeling *nothing*! I found that by feeling "nothing," I felt Him. In losing myself, I found Him. The phrase from the bible: "Be Still—and KNOW—I AM GOD" became so very real. Without thinking, there came a "knowing" of something else inside me. Not my voice—but somehow still mine. Not my thoughts—but somehow still mine, presented to me as a flash of light. That light, that voice, those thoughts penetrated every cell in my being—and I knew I had no choice but to pay attention. To listen. I knew the vague awareness that was beginning to swell in my Soul was the God I had always yearned for but never knew existed. The voice I heard was in the language of God, spoken to my soul as peace and magnificent love.

In hearing this voice, I came to understand that all I believed to be true—wasn't. All I believed to be right or wrong—wasn't. The tendency to think of myself as separate vanished from any perceived reality.

Thinking I was separate from Him had caused me such harm. Now, within this emptying of myself, I learned the truth of His existence and my relationship to that truth. Thoughts seemed to be coming from all directions at once. I had somehow left *me* behind and opened myself up to Him to direct my thoughts, and this brought with it a realization that my usual thinking was full of errors and misconceptions; it was downright ridiculous at times! My thoughts and beliefs just dissolved into the nothingness that they deserved as I realized they were naught but my human need for control over something that wasn't mine to control: the power of life and death itself. That was my surrender—and that became my salvation. My human desire for control was in direct opposition to His wanting to teach me and reveal to me, in love, His very Being within and of me. I had to get out of my own way in order to see Him.

The darkness I had surrounded myself with kept me from seeing who I was...and who He was. I was so Soul-weary; I'd withdrawn from life and from myself. My surrender, my need to end all that I was, brought with it a new emergent sense of something unknown to me. Somehow, I began to see and understand that I was a perfect extension of Him. Realizing that I lived solely because He "thought" of me was impossible to fathom at first. But I began to understand that the very breath I breathed was His—and that if I was a perfect extension of Him, then He lived in me—not somewhere "out there" inaccessible or alien to my Soul. The real me, then—the *true* me—was an attribute of God Himself. Giving up all that I was, or pretended to be; relinquishing all control over my life opened up a new awareness and an awakening seized my Soul just as surely as if someone had reached inside me and pulled my very heart out of my body.

The lesson I had to learn, as do we all, is that we must awaken to our true selves in order to remember and be conscious, once again, of our Divine Self in God and God in us. Leaving behind all the falsities of our human beliefs is essential to the "remembering" of our true nature and where we fit into the tapestry of all life.

Part of my shift was realizing that attaching myself to religious practices and teachings, holding to my own thoughts and beliefs, had kept me blinded from seeing what I instinctively knew. What has been called "the rubbish of life" keeps us from our true nature. I had a lot of rubbish! Pulling aside, for the first time, the veil that separates us from the truth, reveals the transcendent nature that is our birthright. We know this—we just forget it for a while until every fiber of our being quickens with a newly discovered perception of Divine truth.

When I lived in darkness, it seemed way too difficult to leave "the rubbish" behind. And indeed, I was never given a choice; rather, it just became my new reality. Suddenly,

I was living in the light. It felt overwhelming at times—I had all this newfound knowledge but understood very little of it. So my journey of understanding began. I wasn't quite sure where to even begin. I tried desperately to hold onto the feeling of that impossible love and "knowing" that I had experienced in my SDE, but humanity came knocking and that, all by itself, started to strip away that feeling of "completeness of being." I was unable to hang on to that perfection. So I researched people, places, events, anything I could that would help me understand the complexities—and simplicity—of my SDE.

My goal—to go back into that Starlight—was something I feared I could never do, so I told myself if I could just understand all of it, every single bit of it, that would suffice. I knew this thinking would set me on a journey full of consequence and frustration, but I felt compelled to embark on it. I had no idea where to start—so I started exactly where I was! With zero knowledge of the SDE, other than what I had experienced.

I searched out philosophers, priests, teachers of all kinds, gurus, Buddhist monks, Reiki, meditation teachers – all in an attempt to understand and explain my SDE. I was once again inserting my human need for control into an experience that neither needed nor wanted any human personality or opinion. Inserting my own thoughts into my Starry night kept me, once again, on edge and irritated at my own lack of control and inability to find what I was looking for.

I could feel my search wasn't working—so I stopped and went back to basics. I had to somehow become selfless again. But how to do that? Human nature is fueled by ego. And, as a beloved teacher of mine, Dr. Wayne Dyer, said, "ego means edging God out." That self-inflating ego haunts each and every one of us and keeps us from our true awakened self. So, back to basics it was and the basics here came from the Word of God Himself.

So I did return to my childhood faith for a while and started to pore over Scripture in an effort to "recognize" something that would now make more sense. I looked for verses concerning God's abiding love, the God within, God's temple, Holy Spirit indwelling—anything that "felt" familiar to the experiences of my Starry journey. I wanted desperately to relive that moment of surrender when I was "no more." I found myself questioning *everything* about my experience in an effort to relive it. I haunted every religion and every place of worship for hundreds of miles around. Thinking this effort would eventually meet with success, I looked forward to—and yet was anxious about—every new Sunday that would require me to enter into yet another "search."

Try as I might, I couldn't find anything that resembled my Starlit night. It was depressing. In fact, I found that organized religion held little for me anymore – it seemed as if there was no place I fit in. The control they exerted over what one was to believe—never questioning, never looking beneath or beyond for a fuller understanding—didn't set my Soul on fire as did my experience on that Blessed night. But every week, I would return to a community that seemed bent on just accepting, at face value, what the minister had to say.

I recognized my former self in all of them and knew I could not then, nor ever, go back to that particular behavioral pattern. So I left behind that "organized" part of my life and wandered in search of a new landing zone. I knew that a glimpse of my experience was all I needed. I just needed to see it for a split second and then I could remember how to get there!

In my search, I had forgotten that opening myself up completely to Him, emptying myself of all opinion, thought, attitude, and belief was the only way to accomplish my desire to return to His wisdom and share in His love again. I had to remember how to "Be Still...and Know...that I am God." Be still—just stop—just stop! It seemed too simple, too easy. And I had heard it so many times before.

In the end, seeing and hearing that phrase: "Be Still..." through the lens of a new set of beliefs brought a new understanding and helped me find my way back to my Starry night. It wasn't an earth-shattering aha! moment; rather, it was a moment of silence and inner contemplation. It was the only way I could accomplish my desire to unite, once again, with pure light. "Turn inward to me. Let go. You are safe. Let me direct you. Be Still and listen." Taking one deep cleansing breath, letting go of my need to control this and every other event of my life, turned out to be my way back.

Opening my heart and Soul, emptying myself completely, meant giving up on a lifetime of beliefs—but this was necessary for my survival. Old beliefs were replaced by the abiding love of God and the knowledge that I was one with my Creator—not separate or alone.

Letting go of the ego is not an easy thing to do. But it is necessary for awakening to the truth of who you are. You are not ego. You are not your thoughts or desires. They are just concepts that you pretend to love or need; concepts based on something outside of yourself. What you find is the same thing that we all find when we look for comfort or love or contentment or joy outside of ourselves—something unreal and unfulfilling. Of course, achieving any goal makes you feel happy—for a while—but then uneasiness sets in and you're off again to find that "something else" to fill you up. There is no peace in anything outside of yourself—you must look within and find the peace that is there just waiting to fill you up. You must reach out and grasp all that is within you to open up that exhaustless light of love—and wisdom. This should be an easy thing to do for "an awakened soul," right? I found that thought to be nothing but pure ego.

It's not easy to find peace within—not even for those who have experienced an NDE or a SDE. The gift given freely tends to pale when we are forced to perceive the experience through human eyes. When our humanity takes over we, once again, turn to our own thoughts concerning the why's and how's of such an experience. Our humanity doesn't play well with Spiritual perception of such magnitude. Holding onto the reality of who we truly are is hard in a world where temptations and desire, wants and perceived needs get in the way. Even for those who have tasted the reality, peeked behind the veil that leads to truth—it can prove to be quite difficult.

Remembering the one true consciousness is one thing—continually feeling it and living in it is quite another thing altogether. It is only through many failures and a complete loss of strength—and an inability, when ego raises its ugly head, to completely trust that you are not alone—that "turning inward" becomes the resolve of your heart. Learning to "hear," to distinguish His voice from all the noise, can be tricky at best. That was my most hard-fought battle. To this day, I still feel the need to search for my desires by myself, to control my actions without input from anyone. I still forget to "remember" to go within and "Be Still" in order to listen. That is why my SDE, my journey of discovery, has lasted for decades.

Yes, I still search. I still research. I still look for ways to do it all by myself. And I still fail. But one thing I know for certain—I will never again feel alone or abandoned. I will never fail to remember or feel His abiding love and Presence. I will never fail to "Be still and Know" that He lives in me as I live in Him. My awakening begins anew every day as I sit quietly and listen to the reality of what I know for sure—that I am a magnificent extension of my Creator who formed me from a mere thought and then gave life to that thought. I had to come to that awakening, to Him, in complete and utter surrender—defeated and thrashing about in the dark.

My journey from darkness to light was an intensely painful one. I would not heap these pains onto anyone, but I must say that I wouldn't change a thing about my life if it meant my Starlight experience would be lost to me.

And I know, beyond measure or thought, that one day I will be taken back to my Starlight to dwell, once again, in that perfect light, to be engulfed and cocooned in that perfect love that has no description, no beginning, no ending. And I know that it is within "that place" that all boundaries will be lifted and I will, at last, be taken deeper into "that place" I was not allowed to go— where all my loved ones are waiting for me – within the Starlight which, as I discovered, was the very presence of God.

From darkness to light… that place where He and I are one… and pure light lives as unfathomable love— just exactly where is that? I found it in the undeniable completeness of being One with my Creator. I found it in surrender. I found it in remembering what I had forgotten—my awareness of His breath being mine and my breath being His expression in this world. I found it by going "within" and letting go of pretense and illusion and worldly controls. I found it in faith—hard fought and won by Grace. And, as a woman of faith, I found that it was Christ, God Himself, not the priests or rabbis or ministers, that allowed me to see through the glass clearly and find reality in and of God. I found it by learning to listen to—and finally recognize—His voice in me.

God needs a "yes" for Him to do His work in awakening a Soul to the truth. It is simplicity at its best and its worst. The price: giving up who you think you are in order to find who you were meant to be when God smiled at the very thought of you.

Difficult stuff! When I began to understand, in a novice way, the mystic's way of being, I learned that the heart of hearts, inaccessible to anyone or anything except God, through union with Him, was the place I needed to be. In this mystical, magical, secreted away dominion—God's dwelling place—He moves and lives and breathes for us, and it is through this Divine union that we come to the truth of all reality. That reality? That truth? There is not now nor will there ever be a separation from God— unless we separate ourselves by thought or belief that is human frailty and ego. Knowing there is absolutely nothing that God is not, nowhere that He is not, and nothing that He is not a part of, leads you home.

My search has become never-ending. Now I yearn for a union on a deeper level, so each time I hear "Be Still and Know"—I listen. I have found that every time I hear something, it is for my benefit. Sometimes, during my still moments, I can't move forward—but I no longer see this as tedious or frustrating. I know it is only serving to make me stronger and, therefore, more able to comprehend that which is, oftentimes, incomprehensible. I know that once God has accomplished His purpose in and for me—I will, once again, have that complete Divine union that I crave and my search will come to an end.

To be awakened to the very nature of God—to Divine wisdom and truth—is the goal of my existence.

To be awakened to the Soul, to God's consciousness that abides and lives within my heart—I want that. To truly feel the Presence within, just as I felt the Presence in Starlight, is my goal.

Awakening to true Spirit has become a way of living in this world. I am a seeker and, most likely, will remain one. Being taken further and further into His Presence has been the joy of my life. Many of my friends have asked me, sometimes in jest, "What exactly does it feel like to be an "awakened Soul?" My answer is always the same...

"I'll tell you when I meet one!"

CHAPTER 15:
SHOULD I BE AFRAID?

"Should I be afraid?" Every time I'm asked that question, I smile. It's a smile that just touches the corners of my eyes but permeates my entire Soul. I feel complete understanding and sublime melancholy as I look back and remember.

I remember those yesterdays—the ones that live in me still—and I recall falling face first, lying in the muck and mire, my body fueled by the emotions evoked by that question, "Should I be afraid?" I remember so well when the world toppled off its axis and the darkness swallowed me whole, taking with it a lifetime of beliefs and wishes and dreams—leaving me, tormenting me with the question, "Should I be afraid?" I understand that question—the emotion; the numbness; the overriding emptying of the heart; the abject fear that lives in those words; the spiritual detachment that takes your breath away—I understand.

I am asked that question every single day—I hear it from people who, just like me, are or were facing something so terrifying, so fearful that all reason just dissipated into nothingness and left an emotion so cruel, it cannot or could not be named. That question is usually the last one in a string of queries asked by patients and their families after they've been given the life-altering messages that need time to seep into their brains; the messages that strip them of the innocence that was their lives before being confronted with the truth of their mortality. That question is all they want answered when the M.D. leaves them—and I enter. They want someone to "take it all away." They just want an answer, and hope that I can give it to them.

But it's not quite that simple. I could very easily say, "Of course—you have plenty to scare the bejesus out of you!" Or I could take the exact opposite approach and say, "Have faith...just hold onto your faith and believe." Both of those are options—neither of which ever enter my mind when confronted with "Should I be afraid?" That question is only answered on a journey that requires the diminishment of self—a journey that leads to the discovery of one's true purpose within the promise of hope. It's a solitary journey—it must be taken alone. It's deep and dark and requires a strength that won't let go in the midst of the worst trauma and the darkest of all emotion of your life. The journey will take you through the fear of betrayal and separation, the fear of abandonment, the fear of "nothingness," the fear of death—and finally, the ultimate fear: losing yourself to the unknown.

My answer to that question came at great personal expense. Rage and fear left me unable to recognize the very thing that could have ended my struggle, my insatiable need for control over things that no one could ever control. Isolated, I shut myself off and hid behind the walls of a supposed castle that I constructed with stone and steel. I had no faith in anyone or anything. My "aloneness" and grief were better served up cold with solitude and "fakery" and "I'm fine's" than with "Should I be afraid?"—I never, ever would've asked it, even though fear lived for me and through me for all those years. I carried a yoke around my shoulders, much like an ox laboring through life. I knew and believed that there would never be an escape from the pain and suffering that was life itself. And I lied. All the "I'm fine's" and the smiles that never touched my eyes only served to hide the abject fear and betrayal I felt—betrayal on a cosmic level that I had fashioned from my own ignorance and misunderstanding of the one truth that I had never known.

I told myself, "Rise above this, don't let it beat you, get strong … and survive." I would never admit to myself or to anyone else that I felt abandoned … abandoned by the very "thing" that, as a child, I had prayed to every night and said, "If I should die before I wake, I pray the Lord my Soul to take."

Therein lies the crux of the problem. As children, we are invincible. At least, we think we are—if we even think that way at all. We are not taught about death, nor do we discuss it or deal with it or think about it or accept it as part of the "deal." We figure out how to cope with illness, or bad relationships, or job loss, or just plain unhappiness—and we discuss it and debate and argue it and then we just deal with it. But we don't discuss or debate or argue about death on any *real* level. We do talk about death in terms of "what I want or don't want;" we fill out our medical directives and choose our medical proxies "just in case," and then we put those things away and never think of them again. Death and disease happen "to the other guy." We never stop to think that, to that other guy—that's us!

Truly contemplating our own death requires entering into a realm of emotion previously untouched and unacknowledged—a realm protected by that giant "self-preservation" instinct that keeps us safe from the "knowing" that loss of self is even possible. But then denial falls away and what's left is an overriding feeling of betrayal. We feel betrayed by our own bodies, and by the God we prayed to and believed was "watching over us." Previously unknown emotions take the joy out of life and that joy is replaced by unrelenting fear and anxiety, self-doubt and anger, a lack of trust in anything except exactly what is felt at that moment. A complete and overriding separation from a lifetime of perceived reality takes place deep in your Soul—your gut responds, your jaw drops, and the true nature of your humanity emerges: mortality.

In facing shattering loss, I lost all faith in God—the God of my childhood; the God that was preached to me from the pulpit; the God that lived outside of me and supposedly would take care of me if I were "good." A life-and-death diagnosis can make even the most faithful begin to quake and question whether God "hears" them or not; whether He exists or not; whether He is just some invention created to give power and control over the "unwashed masses" to a chosen few.

"Should I be afraid?" is the one question that cannot be glossed over or ignored with simple words or comprehensive explanations regarding upcoming treatments and outcomes. I knew all that during my dark night—and I still fell. Why did I still fall? Because I didn't know how to deal with death. I didn't know how to talk about it or share it or face it. I ran as far and as fast as I possibly could—from myself, from family… and from God. I ran from the God I thought I knew—one who is entirely different from the One Who Knew me, who was just waiting on the other side of my belief in separation—a separation I created and reveled in! Refusing to surrender to the mortality that is inherent in all life instead of facing it down, plowing through it, grabbing it by the throat and introducing myself wholly and fully, with all my flaws and fears upfront and growling—confronting the realities of life—left me alone and running scared for years.

I found that in my pretense of "I'm above all this" and "I'm in control," the fear and pain grew unabated—and I fell. I would not allow God—if He did exist—to break me. Hemingway once wrote, "The world breaks everyone. Those who don't break—die." Having no one to share my grief with, or not wanting to or knowing how to share that grief—did, indeed, break me—but bitterness and my need for some ridiculous existential revenge kept me from seeing that my very salvation was in the hands of the One I ran from.

And so, I smile every single time I am asked, "Should I be afraid?" I smile as I remember my loves—for they are the indwelling's of my Soul...the whispers of my Spirit. I know that every single person asking me that question is about to embark on the most arduous journey of their lives and is struggling—and will continue to struggle—to find his or her own path to some sort of victory, or at least some sort of survival that will make life more tolerable until their new norm finds its way.

It makes me feel such a sublime melancholy, the emotion I never understood until my Soul sorted it all out in the presence of my Creator, a God previously unknown to me. All the human thoughts and downright nonsense that we are exposed to throughout our formative years sticks to us like tar and, once the potholes start to form— the questions force us to rip that tar from our bodies and discover what's underneath it all. It is there, in that "ripping off" process—that fear can be unearthed and sent packing. Being able to peel away the confusion that lives in the mind—the confusion that was slapped on your forehead with all the other labels of expectation— helps rid you of the fear that comes from never knowing yourself as you were meant to be and from simply being alive. Knowing that then allows "sublime melancholia" to change your way of being in the world. Shakespeare called it "sweet sorrow," which always elicits an "Oh...so sad"...but the true meaning of that emotion is found in the uniting of pain and joy into one feeling that, as of yet, has no name. Sublime melancholia, is, then, a mix of pure joy and deep despair, the two smashing into one another with a force so powerful it mimics the big bang theory of life. It's there that empathy and compassion first meet and grow up. It's the emotion that springs to life when you finally access the underside of your Soul—the place where all truth lies hidden. It's the very nature of life itself.

I don't have the answer, the exact words necessary to give to anyone to expel the darkness of fear; only God knows the answer. But He puts that knowledge in each and every Soul created by His very thoughts. It's there, in that heart of hearts, that fear is powerless and cannot live. Why? Because that is the part of you that has always been connected to the truth of who you are—the part of you that exists in and of God. Discovering that life isn't out to get you, that it's just life—and that darkness and death are all part of the stuff of life—is the "thing" that no one wants to talk about or admit.

It's in the dark moments of our lives that our spiritual self is challenged and it's in those very same dark moments that our human, non-spiritual self can emerge and slap us square in the face. We fear becoming "nothing" and we refuse to admit—on any level other than a surface one—that death is even a possibility for us or for someone we love. It is quite impossible to envision ourselves as "not being here" and, being forced to envision this takes us into a world of desperation and intense spiritual and emotional suffering where conflict with everything you have allowed yourself to be, to do, to have, to experience, to love, to hate, to believe—all come into play. Everything you have ever believed in loses its significance and you lose yourself. Denial and shock override religion or reason, theology or philosophy, ideology or purpose. Disillusionment replaces whatever you think you know—and you fall.

Pretending the fear isn't real or expected, pretending there is an absence of tremendous pain in the emotions that jumble themselves together within this "fear package" is extremely damaging. It gives rise to even more anxiety and desperation, which constantly feed upon themselves. This most raw and vulnerable of all emotional states is an unrelenting, savage killer of all things good and kind.

So, how exactly is that question answered? Not in organized religion, nor in philosophical musings or ideologies that put you in a prison of sorts. The answer lies in the journey that begins with the first step that takes you directly into that fear. When you take that step, when you acknowledge that fear, you may start to feel separate and apart from "what was" and closer to "what is."

In arriving at "what is," you may be met with silence. It's a funny thing—that silence. There's the silence that is met when someone has no clue how to act or respond, and then there's the silence of the "knowing" that exists behind the eyes of someone who has been there. But before they get to that place of knowing, the silence behind the eyes appears to be focused not quite on anything in particular but, instead, on everything; or they're fixated on one very small and totally inconsequential "something"—like a dust particle floating in the room, or a single dead leaf on some forgotten plant in the corner. Or like I was—zeroed in on a filament of blue on the Oriental carpet in our oncologist's office – the piece that was just a little thicker than the rest of them. The unknowing eyes are filled with fear, or more accurately—unacknowledged dread.

But if, indeed, the eyes are the windows to the Soul, then what is needed is some "Soul recognition." Silence, and eyes that recognize that silence, bring about an intimacy so profound that words become totally unnecessary. It's the stuff we keep in the deepest recesses of our Soul that speak a language like no other, and are recognized and understood in that moment before words get in the way. The eyes speak for themselves with the tears of hope that mingle with the quiet desperation of loss.

When devastation hits and emptiness follows, hope is oftentimes abandoned—or, just the opposite—hope is paraded across the room, by a family member, on a banner that reads, "I will control this and never be defeated. I will never let go."

There's a funny thing about "letting go"–that's the entrance to the mystery of life. Your intellect won't get you there. Your explanations and understandings of the way the world operates won't get you there. "Letting go" frees you from the sometimes nonsensical dribble of human thought, the explanations of who and what God is and just where you fit into the overall plan. "Letting go" takes you to the very will of the One who created you—and the mystery becomes one that is understood on a level not experienced in everyday life. When God's Grace touches your Soul, fear vanishes in "the twinkling of an eye" and it's then that one can see His hand carefully putting the broken pieces back together, binding them with strands of insight and truth, sublime truth mingled with sadness—humanity defined.

But "letting go" doesn't come easily at first. Why? Because we simply can't envision our future anymore, so we must make it and control it ourselves by any means necessary. In our "before this" time, we think we are prepared and we tell ourselves that we will know "exactly" what to do if ever confronted with some horrendous situation. We don't. We think we have it "all together." We don't. We think we know exactly what to do and exactly how to behave and exactly what to say or where to go for help. We don't. And we think we know what to believe. After all, we've been taught all our lives what to believe in, what's real and good and just. We don't. Fear takes all that away, while anger, anxiety, depression, and hopelessness take the place of certainty and "known truths." I know there are some who tell themselves their "faith" is strong and complete, and fear will never enter the equation, only to be devastated when that very faith encounters the fear inherent in all of humankind.

None of us—not one single person alive—is going to escape the truth of that mortality. We are all going to cause unbearable pain to those who love us just as they will cause us unbearable pain when we lose them.

It's the stuff of life…and love. Expressing those pains and fears is difficult, seemingly impossible in some situations, but vitally important in each and every life ever lived. We all cling to the people we love. We all cling to what we believe is our "life force." We all fight like hell to escape the inescapable—and when we don't escape, or worse still, when someone we love doesn't escape—anger and bitterness and confusion and fear rule the day. Sometimes that fear is expressed in words such as "I have faith" or "God will see us through this." But these words block the very thing that will allow for the "letting go" of that fear. Not allowing yourself to become vulnerable—hiding behind some image of who and what you think you are and who and what you believe God wants you to be—will ultimately destroy you.

For years, the answer was presented to me, and yet I continually tossed it away as I would toss away a crumpled-up dirty cloth that had been used to clean up some filth somewhere that no one wanted to deal with. My answer, my very salvation—recognizing and accepting my very own human frailties—came at last, but it did not come easily. Stripped to my very core, devoid of ego and hope, learning that joy and suffering were bedmates—all of it happened on a hard fought journey into my humanity. I've been bloodied and bruised by my own humanity so many times, the bruises are visible still.

Losing faith and finding God become the very same thing when you permit yourself to fully let go and express the humanity that is screaming to get out and play. Some say getting angry with God is a "bad" thing. I couldn't disagree more. I believe it is a necessary and essential element in meeting Him for the very first time!

So, when I'm asked that question, I answer it in a most peculiar way. I most certainly don't ask for belief in me. I don't ask for belief in my God. I don't ask for belief in any particular religion or set of beliefs. I don't ask for belief in any one physician or any one treatment or even in any one guiding principle of life. Quite the contrary, I ask for an open mind and a questioning heart—free of the constraints that our humanity places on all of us. Constraints that keep us bound to an existence that begins and ends in the here and now, ideas and systems of behavior and beliefs that teach about the permanence or impermanence of life, intellectual reasoning's and "facts" that keep us bound to this physical realm. Going beyond all that is what I ask. I ask for the truth that lies hidden in the heart... hidden in mystery... and hidden behind the eyes.

Confronting that fear, that anger, and that hopelessness can take you to the exact place you need to be. Confronting the frailties that none of us want to confront takes them out of the body and out of the Soul... and what presents itself is the one thing that has been missing, the one thing that we never knew or took the time to know – the God that lives within. Fear cannot survive, cannot exist in the presence of God. When you face yourself, you face God. When you face the reality of all life, you face the true nature that has been lying hidden in plain sight: life, as we know it, exists only in the present. There may be no tomorrow and yesterday has passed into memory. Once awareness wakes up, and we allow ourselves to sit quietly in that fear, we enter into a time where compromise with yourself is impossible and the "letting go" can begin. Some may see "letting go" as giving in and losing all hope. Quite the contrary, the "letting go" is the first step in the journey to the unseen and the unacknowledged truth of life that exists in the very heart of a loving and compassionate God.

There's an old French proverb that says, "He who fears to suffer, suffers from fear." Accepting that fear, acknowledging it and tasting the suffering within it, can lead you to a place beyond any belief system; it can help you break free from the assumptions of others regarding your "truth." This has nothing to do with religion, nor does it have anything to do with the sometimes foolish assumptions mankind makes about God. The mystery of the universe, of God Himself, is so much greater than our human minds could ever comprehend—and hitching our lives to any one explanation of who and what God is leaves us lacking. I presumed to know God. I was wrong. Sometimes it is within tremendous suffering that we find our way to God. It is the acceptance of all that is…in the present…which brings us into the faith we always wanted and the hope that is our birthright.

"It is the end that crowns us…not the fight" (Robert Herrick). Some would say it's the fight that's important.

I say otherwise. It's in the quiet times, when we have no choice but to put down all the baggage and nonsense we use to protect ourselves from the world we live in— that's the important step in the process of "becoming" and finding the truth of our existence. Throwing off that entire pretense and just "being"—that's where we find the peace we need to see ourselves as we truly are: the grand mystery of God Himself.

"Should I be afraid?" Every time I hear that question, I smile. It's a smile that just touches the corners of my eyes but permeates my entire Soul. The fears of the ones who voice it are the echoes of a nightmare I once lived in … and managed to survive. My help came in the form of a Blessing so immense that it changed my entire life for evermore. I have no idea just why I was granted such a Blessing and, most likely, will never know. Were the "remembrances of love" so strong a conviction on Steve's part that the Universe took notice and took me in? Or did God intervene in His own plan and take me to Him because of a plea—or just "because?" I will never know, so I just accept it as part of the great mystery that we all belong to. I use my understanding of that nightmare, that silence, that look hidden just beneath the eyes, that fear and confusion, that overwhelming primal scream that only God can hear … I use the experiences of my nightmare to understand theirs. I use my past terrors to get into theirs. I use my silence to help them through theirs. I use my hands to wipe away the same tears that fell from my eyes when no one else was watching. I use my pain to help them understand theirs … so they know that they are not alone.

Giving them—all of them—my Starlit night, in hopes they will understand that they are part of all Creation; part of something they do not fully understand; part of something so much bigger than themselves; part of something they cannot see or hear or touch or even imagine; part of something that never left them nor ever could; that they are part of God Himself, part of the true design and permanence of all that has ever been or ever will be, bound to the unimagined intrinsic part of all creation—Starlight itself and the Presence Within that has no comparison, no judgment, nothing but compassion beyond all reason—that is the goal.

"Should I be afraid?" is the most important question asked—and answered—truthfully and gently, for fear of losing ourselves to the unknown is the "thing" that haunts our every thought. It is not only the stuff of nightmares, but also the stuff of an unacknowledged waking dream that leaves no one untouched.

So man, woman or child—I gather them to myself, wipe their tears from their questioning eyes as I whisper...

"Let me tell you a story"......

And so ... the journey begins ...

EPILOGUE

A few short weeks before my dad passed from this world, he pulled me aside and said "Honey, I need to talk to you." As I knelt down beside him, my mind drifted back to my childhood when I would kneel at his side waiting in anticipation for a story that would both amaze and delight me. Somehow, I knew this was not going to be one of those stories.

"Honey, do you remember when, right before we would get transfer orders, I would gather you girls together and talk about what was about to happen? That I was going to leave, and then you all would join me?" he said, smiling down at me. My heart froze at his words and I looked away lest he see the tears that were welling up in my eyes. He spoke again, "Honey, look at me." So, once again, I looked up into the eyes of the man that, to this day, even though I am a grown-ass woman, I still refer to as "Daddy," and listened to his goodbye.

"Going away is never easy, sweetheart, but remember I'm not going away for long—I'm just going ahead to get everything ready for you and your mom and sisters to come." You remember that and tell your sisters to remember that too. I'm just going ahead like I always have."

He left us right before Christmas as I held his hand and looked straight into his eyes and told him, "Go find Steve and Stephanie, Daddy. Go."

My dad and I talked at length, many times, about that Starlit night and how it changed our entire universe of belief. Nothing in our lives, in my life, ever taught me even one iota as much as my time in "that place" and nothing has ever left me with more questions about life than my SDE. The one question that I am asked more than any other, not only by others but also by me, myself is, "What'd ya learn out there?"

When asked that question I always answer, "I learned about life—from Death. Death taught me more than any professor or confessor ever had–which is still true today. Death was, and always will be, my greatest teacher."

Why was Death my greatest teacher? Because it was within Death that I found life. To say that I found Life in death may sound confusing to some. But it took Death to expose the truth of the universe. And that truth was so simple—one I would have never admitted to in my need for that existential revenge I had sought against God for "doing this to us."

So what did I learn? I learned that, in trying to orchestrate our lives by myself, I had opened myself up for failure. I had written my story, our story, and had closed the book on any edits—never once considering the fact that problems are inescapable. They are the richness, the depth, the intertwining threads of the tapestry that is our mortal life, and no matter how hard we try to push them away or run from them or manage every aspect of them—we are all incapable of controlling them. The life and death problems that expose our human limitations and frailties—they are what life is all about! I found that any strength or abilities I had—ones that I assumed would "make it all better"—were useless, which became glaringly evident as time passed and I became more helpless every day. The aridity of my life was made abundantly clear when I found myself in the presence of my Creator. Tending to immediately go into "control mode" or "fix-it mode" is in my nature. It is an automatic response for me—one that I still run to today instead of doing the exact opposite, what I know I should do—turning to silence and "being still." For it's in that silence and in that "being still" that I find my answers and my strength.

Within that stillness, I find the very same Presence that made Itself known to me within the stars – and it's there that I come close, once again, to the experiential knowledge of His Reality. It's in "that place" that I learned that chance simply does not control the happenings of His universe. It may seem that the randomness and happenstance of events all point to a world in chaos—but the opposite is true. God is in absolute control of all things and whether we like it or not, our human understanding of His ways is equivalent to that of an amoeba trying to understand the inner workings of quantum theory.

I also learned to face the emptiness that haunted my Soul. Instead of running away from it—I leaned in to embrace it. For within that emptiness I found the one thing that could fill me to brimming—His constant and abiding love for me. He had always been there—hurting when I hurt, weeping when I wept and—unknown to and unwanted by me—carrying me in His arms when I fell.

Perhaps the greatest lesson of all would be this—I learned to trust in the abiding Presence and love of God that is ever-constant even in the darkest of times and in the cataclysms of my life. I learned to lean into His limitless love and power. Yes, I still rage and scream and shake my fist at the heavens when I feel completely overwhelmed and afraid and I try, every single day, to enter into the prayer that is the most difficult of all prayers—"Your will, not mine"—and still fail miserably as I add my own "P.S...but I sure would like it my way!" It's then I can hear Him: "Are you at it again?" as He chuckles at me because He knows my heart. He knows my heart—He always did—a gift handed to me in Starlight. A gift I will never forget again.

So, I sit in His Presence, in the silence that isn't silent because He speaks to my heart of hearts in "that place"...and says, "follow me...this way, Sharon." "Whether you turn to the right or to the left, your ears will hear a voice behind you, saying, 'This is the way: walk in it' "...Isaiah 30:21.

He is my refuge and my strength. I know that now and will never turn from Him even when I feel like running in the opposite direction because I don't understand the purpose behind something that seems to be an utter calamity. I constantly remind myself that I am safe with him and that His plan for me—although one I cannot fathom and may not want to endure—is perfect. He created it for me before all time, and it is perfect.

Crawling inside the bowels of fear, only to have Death spirit me back home to "that place" where love was born and where darkness never enters.... instilled in me an ever-present question. I cursed His name. I denied his existence. I belittled those who had faith in Him. And yet, He took me in his arms. So I ask, "Why me, Lord? Why me?"

I would love to say that my SDE has made my life perfect, has made me unafraid of all things that go bump in the night and has me laughing at death when it comes so stealthfully that I feel it staring holes in my Soul. But I can't say that. I still feel fear and anger and, as much as I don't want to admit it, I still have moments of extreme "Why are you doing this to me?" I would love to say that I have gone beyond all these human weaknesses and frailties, but that would be an outright lie of immense proportion! I would love to say I have found the answers to all of life's questions—but I can't. As a matter of fact, I have more questions now than ever before! My SDE has resulted in a journey with a host of question marks emblazoned across it and is one that will last my entire lifetime. I may not ever receive an answer to the exact question that lives in my heart and I don't know if that is truly the right question I should be asking, but I will keep searching for the answer.

I may never return to Starlight while I am on this earth. I accept that. There may never be another invitation to return home to "that place" until I return to stay in His Presence for all eternity. I accept that. And while I may rage and scream and shake my fist at the heavens—and constantly question His plan—I do it all the while knowing that He is with me always. Even during those times when I can't feel His Presence, I know He is either pushing me along, holding me up or walking right beside me.

My dad always used to say, "Just let it go, honey. Just let it go and let God." I never knew just how to do that.

I was Blessed with the answer of exactly how to do that when God sent the stars to gather me to Him. So now I just say "Come and get it."

And He does...

Suggested Reading

Glimpses of Eternity: Sharing a Loved One's Passage from this Life to the Next by Raymond A. Moody, M.D. with Paul Perry (Guideposts, 2010)

Life After Life: The Bestselling Original Investigation That Revealed "Near-Death Experiences" by Raymond A. Moody, M.D. (HarperOne, Anniversary edition, 2015)

The Light Beyond: New Explorations by the Author of Life after Life by Raymond A. Moody, M.D. (Rider & Co., 2005)

Map of Heaven: How Science, Religion and Ordinary People are Proving the Afterlife by Eben Alexander, M.D. (Simon & Schuster, 2014)

Evidence of the Afterlife: The Science of Near Death Experiences by Jeffrey Long with Paul Perry (HarperOne, 2010)

The Transformative Power of Near-Death Experiences: How the Messages of NDEs Can Positively Impact the World by Penny Sartori, Ph.D. and Kelly Walsh (Watkins, 2017)

Appointments with Heaven: The True Story of a Country Doctor's Healing Encounters with the Hereafter by Dr. Reggie Anderson with Jennifer Schuchman (Tyndale Momentum, 2013)

Somewhere In Between: The Hokey Pokey, Chocolate Cake and the Shared Death Experience by Lizzie Miles (Trail Angel Press, 2011)

Made in the USA
Middletown, DE
09 July 2018